Lecture Notes in Computer Science   3128

Commenced Publication in 1973
Founding and Former Series Editors:
Gerhard Goos, Juris Hartmanis, and Jan van Leeuwen

Dmitri Asonov

Querying Databases Privately

A New Approach to Private Information Retrieval

Springer

Author

Dmitri Asonov
IBM Almaden Research Center
650 Harry Road, San Jose, CA 95123, USA
E-mail: dasonov@us.ibm.com

Dissertation der Humboldt Universität zu Berlin
Tag der mündlichen Prüfung: 7. Juli 2003

Referent: Prof. Johann-Christoph Freytag, Ph.D., Humboldt Universität zu Berlin
Referent: Prof. Oliver Günther, Ph.D., Humboldt Universität zu Berlin
Referent: Rakesh Agrawal, Ph.D., IBM Almaden Research Center

Library of Congress Control Number: 2004094685

CR Subject Classification (1998): H.3, H.2, H.4, K.4, K.6.5, C.2

ISSN 0302-9743
ISBN 3-540-22441-6 Springer-Verlag Berlin Heidelberg New York

Springer-Verlag is a part of Springer Science+Business Media

springeronline.com

© Springer-Verlag Berlin Heidelberg 2004
Printed in Germany

Typesetting: Camera-ready by author, data conversion by Olgun Computergrafik
Printed on acid-free paper   SPIN: 11018001   06/3142   5 4 3 2 1 0

Foreword

The Internet and the World Wide Web (WWW) play an increasingly important role in our today's activities. More and more we use the Web to buy goods and to inform ourselves about cultural, political, economical, medical, and scientific developments. For example, accessing flight schedules, medical data, or retrieving stock information become common practice in today's world. Many people assume that there is no one who "watches" them when accessing this data.

However, sensitive users who access electronic shops (e-shops) might have observed that this assumption often is not true. In many cases, E-shops track the users' "access behavior" when browsing the Web pages of the e-shop thus deriving "access patterns" for individual shoppers. Therefore, this knowledge on access behavior and access patters allows the system to tailor access to Web pages for that user to his/her specific needs in the future. This tracking of users might be considered harmless and "acceptable" in many cases. However, in cases when this information is used to harm a person - for example about the person's health problems - or to violate his/her privacy (for example finding out about his/her financial situation), he/she would like to be sure that such tracking is impossible to protect the user's rights.

These simple examples clearly demonstrate the necessity to shield the user from such spying **to protect his/her privacy**. That is, a user should be able to access a database (or a data source in general) without allowing others to "observe" which data is requested and accessed by the user; neither the query nor the answer should be visible or accessible to others. Surprisingly, despite the urgent need for concepts and techniques to protect the user from being spied on, very few results are known and available that addresses the problem adequately. During the last 10 years the area of **Private Information Retrieval (PIR)** has addressed some of the problems concerning privacy. However many of those results are of theoretical nature and thus do not carry over into practical solutions for protecting privacy when accessing information sources on the Web or in databases.

With this book Dr. Asonov is one of the first researchers who addresses the topic of querying data privately in a systematic and comprehensive way developing practical solutions in the context of database systems. The results presented in this book sometimes might look theoretical, but they describe his clear understanding of the problem as well as the solutions required for "real-world" settings, in particular for scalable database solutions. As a basis Dr. Asonov first presents the framework for privately accessing database by developing several algorithms which also include the use of special hardware. In the second part of the book he focuses on solving several important subproblems; for them he also includes some validation by benchmarking to show to efficiency of the solutions. Finally, Dr. Asonov shows how his solutions could be used in solving some problems in the area of voting and digital rights management. Initially, these problems seem to be completely unrelated to PIR, however Dr. Asonov shows how some of his results can be used for creative solutions in the areas mentioned. Overall, the careful reader will notice that - despite the many technical details -his in-depth treatment of privacy in database provides the insight into the problem necessary for such an important topic.

In summary, with this book Dr. Asonov provides a systematic treatment of the problem how to access databases privately. The way he approaches the problem and how he develops solutions makes this book valuable for both researchers and practitioners who are interested in better understanding the issues. He develops scalable solutions that are necessary and important in the context of private information retrieval/private database access. The in-depth presentation of the algorithms and techniques is enlightening to students and a valuable resource for computer scientists. I predict that this book will provide the "starting point" for others to perform further research and development in this area.

Prof. Johann-Christoph Freytag, Ph.D., May 2004

Preface

People often retrieve information by querying databases. Designing databases that allow a user to execute queries *efficiently* is a subject that has been investigated for decades, and is now often regarded as a "researched to death" topic. However, the evolution of information technologies and society makes the database area a consistent source of new, previously unimaginable research challenges. This work is dedicated to partially meeting one of these new challenges: querying databases *privately*.

This new challenge is due to a very fundamental constraint of the conventional concept of querying information. Namely, in the conventional setting, the one who queries (the user) must reveal the query content and, by implication, the result of querying to the one who processes the query (the database server). This constraint seems to be negligible if the user trusts the server. However, the growing population of information providers makes it extremely difficult for users to establish and rely on the trustworthiness of information providers. Indeed, more and more cases are reported wherein information providers misuse the information provided by users' queries against the users, for example by sharing this information with third parties without permission, or by using this information for unsolicited advertisement.

We approach this constraint in a direct manner: If it is difficult to trust the server, we could try to remove the need for trust completely, by hiding the content of the user query and result from the server. This research problem, called Private Information Retrieval (PIR), has been under intensive and mainly theoretical investigation since 1996. These results are classified and analyzed in the first of four parts of this book. Our main contribution is considering this problem from a practical angle, as follows.

In Part II, we accept the assumptions and simplifications made in previous related work, and focus on obtaining efficient solutions and algorithms without changing the common model. Namely, we break the established belief that the server must read the entire database for a PIR protocol to answer a query. We further develop our solution by improving the processing and preprocessing complexities of our PIR protocol.

In Part III we extend the common PIR model in two directions. First, we relax the requirement that no information about a query must be revealed. This allows us to offer the user a trade-off between the level of privacy required and the response time for a query. The second extension of the model is done by understanding the economics associated with the PIR problem. Namely, we assumed that information in the database is from different owners. We then consider the problem of distributing royalties between the information owners, given that no information about content of user queries is revealed.

A number of questions remain to be answered before the problem of querying databases privately can be regarded as completely investigated. However, we argue that results presented in the book have pushed the state of the art in this area, from the entirely theoretical level to the stage where implementing an applicable prototype can be considered ultimately possible.

Acknowledgements

I am most indebted to Professor Johann-Christoph Freytag for the success of this work. Our interaction was an example of a brilliant collaboration between a student and an adviser, so rarely found in science.

I was lucky to secure Professor Oliver Günther as my second advisor. I learned a lot from him. Professor Günther naturally supplemented the image of a perfect professor that I perceived from my first advisor.

I am very grateful to Rakesh Agrawal from IBM Almaden Research Center for being an external reviewer of my dissertation. Professor Sean W. Smith and Alex Iliev from Dartmouth College, Ronald Perez from IBM T. J. Watson Research Center, Christian Cachin from IBM Zürich Research Laboratory, and Frank Leymann from IBM Laboratory Böblingen were my occasional, but nevertheless most valuable external contacts.

I could not survive the hardship of making a Ph.D. without the warm, social support from my graduate school colleagues, and the team of DBIS department of Humboldt University. Especially, I would like to thank Markus Schaal and Christoph Hartwich for our fruitful collaboration in CS research, and my officemates Felix Naumann and Heiko Müller, who had to listen to my erroneous German every day. Ulrike Scholz and Heinz Werner have made DBIS a very comfortable place to work at.

My russian–speaking friends in Berlin, Stanislav Isaenko, Viktor Malyarchuk, and Mykhaylo Semtsiv helped me better understand research as a process by sharing their experiences in biological and physical research.

My teachers in Moscow provided the educational background from which I am benefiting now. Among them Yulia A. Azovzeva, Alexei I. Belousov, Valeri M. Chernenki, Maria T. Lepeshkina, Sergei V. Nesterov, Valentina P. Strekalova, Sergei A. Trofimov, and Valeri D. Vurdov were most helpful.

Last but not least, I am thankful to my family who supported me all the way through.

This research was supported by the German Research Society, Berlin-Brandenburg Graduate School in Distributed Information Systems (DFG grants no. GRK 316 and GRK 316/2).

Table of Contents

Part I

Introduction and Related Work

1 Introduction

In Section 1.1 we provide both informal and formal definitions of the Private Information Retrieval problem. Section 1.2 lists the questions associated with PIR that we answer in this book. Section 1.3 provides examples that motivate research in the area of PIR.

1.1 Problem Statement

The existence of the Private Information Retrieval problem is due to a fundamental constraint of conventional querying. Namely, if one person, Tom, wants to query something from another person, Bob, then Tom *must* reveal the query content to Bob. For example, in a shop, the customer *must* tell the seller what he wants to buy. This fundamental constraint is so natural and so freely accepted by human beings, that no one had ever thought of overcoming it until it recently actually became necessary. By overcoming the constraint, we mean solving a problem of querying without revealing the content of the query. A simplified version of this problem bears the name "Private Information Retrieval" problem (PIR), also alternatively called the "querying databases privately" problem within this book (Figure 1.1). Numerous motivating examples of applications that may benefit from a PIR solution will be presented in Section 1.3. In this section, let us concentrate on stating the problem.

The "querying databases privately" problem sketched in Figure 1.1 appears to be very difficult to solve for several reasons. Among them are uncertainty about what kind of information is retrieved and what type of queries must be answered. To simplify the problem, the initial work on PIR proposes simple models for both the structure of information stored in a database and the structure of user queries [CGKS95]. These models have been widely accepted and used by nearly every study on PIR. The information stored in a database is assumed to be a one-dimensional array of N records (L bits for each record). The query structure is assumed to be of type "return the i-th record" (Figure 1.2).

D. Asonov: Querying Databases Privately, LNCS 3128, 3–10, 2004.

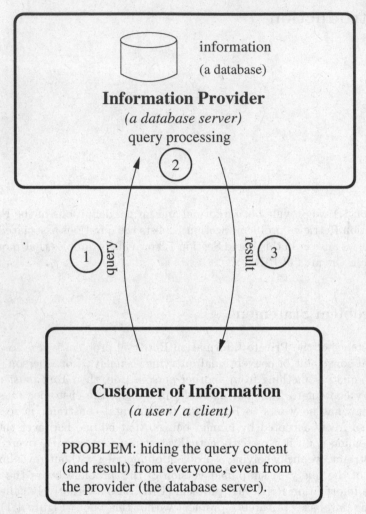

Fig. 1.1. The problem of querying databases privately.

There are several ways to formally define the PIR problem. We present the most readable and easy-to-use variant. However, this necessitates some informality. For stricter definitions, please refer to the works cited in Section 2.2.1.

Definition 1.1.1 (Private Information Retrieval). *Private information retrieval (PIR) is a general problem of* privately *retrieving the i-th record from an N-record array stored on the server. "Privately" means that the server does not know about i, that is, the server does not learn which record the user is interested in.*

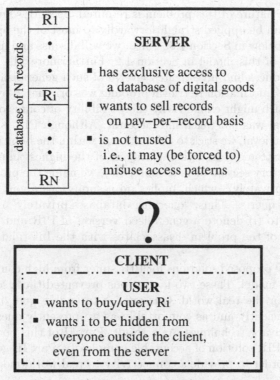

Fig. 1.2. The model for PIR problem.

The informality of the definition above is in the words "does not know about i". Defining this formally requires some effort, and will be done in Chapter 3. There is no need for a more formal definition until then.

An assumption implied by the definition is that the user already knows which record (record number i) to retrieve. We also presume for this model that, from an economical perspective, there is only one price for processing any query. That is, the price for a user retrieving a record does not depend on the identity of the record. Otherwise it would be difficult for the server (the information provider) to bill the user while possessing no information about the content of the query by definition.

There are three remarks regarding the simplicity of the PIR model[1]. First, the model is not oversimplified. As can be seen from the following chapters, approaching solutions for this simple model is a very challenging and complicated task. Before suggesting more complex models, a complete understand-

---

[1] By the simplicity of the PIR model we mean that in this model, (i) the data is presented not as a relational database, but as a plain array of records and (ii) the queries are not of, for example, SQL type but of "return the i-th record" type.

ing of the basic nature of this problem is required. Second, solutions for this simple model can be applied straightforwardly to most of the application areas mentioned below in Section 1.3. Third, we will discuss and motivate some generalizations of this model in Section 1.2. Furthermore, the third part of this book introduces and investigates several of such generalizations.

The Private Information Retrieval problem was originated by the security community, which might explain why the possibility of confusion with Information Retrieval was not taken into account. Although PIR is unrelated to Information Retrieval, we stick to this notation within the book in order to be consistent. In extreme cases, when clarity is of the highest importance (like in this introductory section or in a book title), we name the problem "querying databases privately", which implies no assumptions about the database model nor user queries. Thus, "querying databases privately" is a term that we introduced to (i) denote a generalized version of PIR and (ii) to assure that the name of the problem disassociates with the Information Retrieval research area.

The initially proposed solutions for PIR suffer from high complexities and a minimal PIR model. These two limitations prevented those solutions from being applied in the real world. Our goal is to enable querying databases privately as efficiently and as comfortably as we presently query databases, without any privacy techniques. As a result, Part II of this book focuses on constructing a PIR solution of acceptable complexity. Part III generalizes the PIR model in order to provide a connectivity to real-world models.

1.2 Book Outline

In this section we enumerate the issues that motivated each of the following chapters and our results in solving these issues. Chapters 3 through 5 deal with issues associated with the conventional PIR model. Chapters 6 and 7 generalize the PIR model for the sake of efficiency or practical applicability, respectively.

1. Issue: After analyzing the previous work on PIR [Aso01], we found that all PIR solutions possess $O(N)$ complexities in either query response time [KO97, CMS99, SS00, SS01, KY01] or communication between the information provider (the server) and the user [BDF00, SJ00]. Specifically, in order to answer one query, the database server must read through the entire database of N records, or the amount of information comparable with the database size must be communicated between the server and the user. Both cases are intolerable from the system point of view, as well as from that of the user. In order to be practical, a PIR solution must provide $O(1)$ query response time and $O(1)$ communication.

Result [AF01, AF02a]: In Chapter 3 we propose a PIR protocol with $O(1)$ query response time and communication. It is easy to show[2] that without a preprocessing phase, a query response time smaller than $O(N)$ is impossible. Our solution requires a preprocessing phase of complexity $O(N^2)$, and this preprocessing algorithm must be executed periodically. Furthermore, we use Shannon theory of information [Sha48] to define and to formally prove the privacy property of our protocol.

2. Issue: A) The protocol proposed in Chapter 3 implies a periodical preprocessing wherein the server performs $O(N^2)$ I/Os. In a practical scenario, such preprocessing may take weeks. B) Although our solution provides for $O(1)$ query response time, the response time is not constant and is instead growing linearly with the number k of answered queries.

Result [AF02b]: A) Chapter 4 demonstrates a preprocessing protocol with $O(N^{1.5})$ complexity. In practice, this reduces weeks of preprocessing to hours. B) We expose the fact that the query response time can be reduced from $O(1) = k$ to a constant. This reduction is implemented by applying the preprocessing algorithm mentioned above, given that there is enough time between queries for a preprocessing of $O(k^{1.5})$ complexity.

3. Issue: In related work we found an algorithm of $O(Nlog^2N)$ complexity as an alternative to our $O(N^{1.5})$ preprocessing algorithm. To determine which one has the best performance in practice, we prototyped both algorithms and analyzed the results of extensive, long-running experiments.

Result: In Chapter 5, after analyzing the experimental data we were able to conclude that A) our algorithm outperforms the one from related work by approximately one order of magnitude (for the tested interval $64 \le N \le 2048$), B) the exact complexity of our algorithm lies between $O(N)$ and $O(N^{1.5})$ depending on N, L, and the page size of secondary storage.

4. Issue: All previous PIR algorithms reveal absolutely no information about the content of the query and its result. That is, full privacy is one of the properties of the conventional PIR model. However, the possibility of reducing high complexities of PIR protocols by gradually relaxing the privacy requirement has never been investigated.

Result [AF02c]: In Chapter 6 we propose an algorithm that offers the user a choice in the trade-off between the protocol complexity and the amount of privacy provided.

5. Issue: One of the simplifying assumptions of the PIR model is that no royalties are paid to the producers of the digital goods (product owners). Otherwise, it is unclear how the income should be distributed between the product owners, because no information about identities of the products sold is revealed.

Result [ASF01]: Chapter 7 generalizes the PIR model, whereby it removes the assumption mentioned above. We show that, if we are to dis-

---

[2] The proof is in Chapter 2, Section 2.2.5.

tribute the royalties, the privacy of users can be preserved under certain conditions. First, the function that calculates the royalties must be non-deterministic. Second, we exhibit the only acceptable pattern for such a function. Our work on this problem appears to be of independent interest, bringing a new insight into the research area of secure electronic voting.

1.3 Motivating Examples

We offer two types of examples. First, we enumerate several real-world examples of misuse of the user query content by information providers. These abuses of user privacy, which actually took place, motivate the research in the area of PIR in order to eliminate the possibility of them recurring. Second, we present general application areas where PIR would help.

1.3.1 Examples of Violation of User Privacy

One of the biggest on-line media traders stated that its database containing millions of user profiles and shopping preferences is one of the company's assets. Therefore, this database can be a subject of a commercial deal, i.e., the database can basically be sold to another company without the users' permission [RS00, CNN00]. If the content of user queries were hidden from this information provider, there would no information for him, like user preferences, to sell.

The situation could be even worse to control in the case where the information provider is characterized as "honest but stupid". In other words, information providers may be unaware of flaws in their security levels, thus allowing an intruder to access user preferences collected from the content of their queries. Up to half of the leading on-line information providers are reported to compromise user privacy in such a way [Rot99, Ols99]. If no information about user queries were revealed to a provider, this would solve the problem.

In yet another scenario, information providers may be forced to misuse user preferences. For example, one company was forced to *sell* its database of user preferences due to bankruptcy [Bea00, San00, Dis00]. A more up-to-date list of similar privacy violations can be found in [AKSX02].

In summary, the security of information contained in user queries depends on the good faith of the information provider answering the queries, the quality of the provider's security tier, and the financial situation of the provider. There are too many assumptions that have to be upheld, both simultaneously and forever. Moreover, the number of examples where these assumptions are broken grows from year to year. This leads to the idea of solving the problem in principle – by hiding the content of user queries from everyone, even the one who answers the queries (the information provider).

Solutions to the PIR problem would make it possible for a user to keep the content of his queries private from everybody, including the information provider (sometimes referenced as *server* below).

1.3.2 Application Areas for PIR

In the following, we describe concrete as well as hypothetical examples where PIR protocols might be useful. To some extent, all these application areas are different examples of trading digital goods.

Patent Databases. If the patent server knows which patent the user is interested in, this could cause problems for the user if the user is a researcher, inventor, or investor. Imagine if a scientist discovers a great idea, for example, that "2+2=4". Naturally, he wants to patent it. But first, he checks at an international patent database to see whether such patent or a similar patent already exists. The administrator of that server has access to the scientist's query "Are there patents similar to 2+2=4", and this automatically gives him the following information:

- That "2+2=4" may possibly be an invention. Why not to try to patent it first?
- The research area in which the scientist is working is also notable.

Both observations are highly critical and should not be revealed. PIR solves this problem: The user may pay for downloading a single patent with his credit card (and thus reveal his identity), and the server will not know which patent the user has just downloaded.

Pharmaceutical Databases. Usually, pharmaceutical companies are specialized either in inventing drugs, or in gathering information about the basic components and their properties (pharmaceutical databases). The process of synthesizing a new drug requires information on several basic components from these databases. To hide the plans of the company, drug designers buy the entire pharmaceutical database. These huge expenses could be avoided if the designers used a PIR protocol, allowing them to only buy the information about the few basic components [Wie00].

Media Databases. These are commercial archives of digital information, such as electronic publications, music (mp3) files, photos, or video. As shown above, it can be risky to trust an information provider with customer data. In this context, the user may be interested in hiding his preferences from the server while buying one of the digital products online. This means that the user may be interested in a PIR protocol.

Academic Examples. Suppose that the Special Operations department of the defense ministry is planning an operation in region R. In order to get a high-resolution map of R, this department must make an appropriate request to the IT department's map database. Thus, the IT department's staff could figure out that there will be a special operation in the region R soon. Is it possible to keep the secret inside the Special Operations department and still let a query to be processed at the external database? It is generally possible, if PIR is used [Smi00].

Another hypothetical application is suggested by Isabelle Duchesnay [BCR86]. A spy disposes of a corpus of various state secrets. In his catalogue, each secret is advertised with a tantalizing title, such as "Where is Abu Nidal". He would not agree to give away two secrets for the price of one, or even partial information on more than one secret. You (the potential buyer) are reluctant to let him know which secret you wish to acquire, because his knowledge of your specific interests could be a valuable secret for him to sell to someone else (under the title: "Who is Looking for Terrorists"). You could *privately retrieve* the secret of your choice using PIR, and both parties can remain happy.

There are further real-world examples from biological and medical databases, and the databases of stock information. The bottom line of this section is this: There are enough real-world problems that could be eliminated if an efficient PIR solution (or algorithm) was available.

2 Related Work

In Section 2.1, we demonstrate that solving the PIR problem is not a straight-forward task. Sections 2.2 provides an all-out overview of PIR approaches, and also reviews some work that indirectly relates to PIR. In Section 2.3 we analyze the previous section to establish the problems that remain to be solved, and map these to the following parts of the book.

2.1 Naive Approaches Do Not Work

There are at least two straightforward approaches to the PIR problem (Figure 2.1). Both fail to solve the real-world problem. However, they show what kind of properties the practical PIR solutions must have.

Encryption of Communication. Conventional encryption of a query and its result would prevent third parties from accessing the content of the query and the result as they travel through a communication channel between the client and server. However, the problem is not solved: The content of the query and its result still must be presented in cleartext to the information provider.

Entire Database Download. Theoretically speaking, the entire database transfer (from the server to the client) solves the PIR problem: The client can process queries on his local copy of the database. Thus, the server is unaware of the content of the user queries, and consequently, the server is unaware of the user preferences.

This approach cannot be applied in reality, because of the great cost the user has to pay for all of the records of the database. An additional cost is communication, which is equal to the size of the database. But this cost is usually negligible in comparison to the cost of purchasing the entire database content.

2.2 PIR Approaches

Over 30 scientific papers have been published on the PIR subject since the PIR problem had been formulated in [CGKS95]. We classify the results ac-

D. Asonov: Querying Databases Privately, LNCS 3128, 11–20, 2004.
© Springer-Verlag Berlin Heidelberg 2004

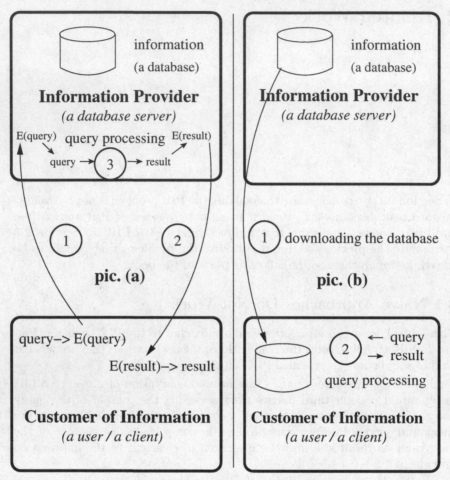

Fig. 2.1. The straightforward approaches are: (a) encryption of the communication and (b) entire database download.

cording to the assumptions that authors rely on in these papers. Algorithms are not explained due to space limitations. Instead, basic ideas of some of the algorithms are given.

2.2.1 Theoretical Private Information Retrieval

In theoretical PIR, the user privacy is unbreakable[1] independently from any intractability assumptions (that is, independently from the computational power of a cheater). Chor et al. prove that any Theoretical PIR solution has a communication with a lower bound equal to the database size [CGKS95].

---
[1] The user privacy is unbreakable iff the content of his queries cannot be revealed.

Thus, downloading the entire database is an optimal solution with respect to the communication amount. Such a solution is called trivial. Consequently, a non-trivial PIR solution is one that has a communication amount less than the database size.

With the idea in mind of getting a non-trivial Theoretical PIR solution, Chor et al. relax the problem setting. They assume that there are several (instead of one) database servers storing the same data and not communicating with each other. This assumption makes a non-trivial Theoretical PIR feasible.

The very basic idea in [CGKS95] is to send several queries to several databases. The queries are constructed in such a way, that they give no information to the servers about the record that the user is interested in. But, using the answers from the queries, the user can construct the desired record.

An additional type of theoretical PIR is considered , when up to t servers are allowed to cooperate against the user.

Ambainis [Amb97] improves the results of Chor et al., and demonstrates the following non-trivial Theoretical PIR solutions:

1. A k database PIR solution (i.e., a PIR solution with k identical databases not communicating with each other), for any constant $k \geq 2$, with communication complexity $O(N^{1/(2k-1)})$.
2. A $\Theta(\log N)$ database solution with communication complexity $O(\log^2 N * \log \log N)$.

Further research on Theoretical PIR appears in [IK99, Ito99, Mis00, Ray00, BDS00, Yam01, BI01, Ito01, BS02, BIKR02, GKST02, YXB02, BFG02]. Quantum Private Information Retrieval is a related problem setting, first mentioned in [KdW02].

PIR of Blocks. PIR of blocks is an extension of a PIR problem. Database records are assumed to be blocks of several (instead of one) bits. Theoretical PIR of blocks is introduced in [CGKS95] and further investigated in [CGN97, Gil00]. Techniques for PIR of blocks are important for making PIR practical. The cases for blocks were also partially considered in those papers mentioned in the next sections. Alternatively, the term "block" may be denoted by "record".

2.2.2 Computational Private Information Retrieval

In order to obtain lower communication complexity, another assumption was weakened by Chor and Gilboa [CG97]. "Computational" means that the observer (the server) is presumed to be computationally bounded. That is, under an appropriate intractability assumption the database servers cannot gain information about i. For every $\varepsilon > 0$, Chor and Gilboa present a two database Computational PIR scheme with communication complexity $O(N^{\varepsilon})$.

In [OS97] Ostrovsky and Shoup construct PIR protocols with the option to write i-th record at the database in a way that the database servers do not know about i. There are protocols both for the Theoretical PIR and Computational PIR, with two or more servers. For example, for Theoretical PIR with three servers, they offer a protocol with communication complexity $O(N^{1/3} \log^3 N)$. The Computational PIR protocol with poly-logarithmic communication complexity requires $O(\log N)$ rounds in comparison to one round for most PIR schemes presented in this chapter.

Computational PIR with a Single Database. The first paper on PIR proved that the Theoretical PIR problem has no non-trivial solutions for the case of a single database. Surprisingly, the substitution of an information-theoretic security with an intractability assumption allows to achieve a non-trivial PIR protocol for a single database schema [KO97]. Its communication complexity is $O(N^\varepsilon)$ for any $\varepsilon > 0$. They use an intractability assumption, described in [GM84]. The basic approach is to encrypt a query in such a way that the server can still process it using special algorithms. However, the server recognizes neither the clear-text query nor the result. The result can only be decrypted by the client. This was also a first single-database protocol, where designers consider and provide database privacy (please refer to Section 2.2.3).

Using another intractability assumption [CMS99], Cachin et al. demonstrated a single database Computational PIR protocol that has polylogarithmic communication. This is an improvement in comparison to polynomial communication complexity in [KO97]. This result looks particularly effective, because the user has to send at least $\log N$ bits just to address the i-th bit (the bit he wants to receive) in the database, independently from whether the protocol preserves privacy or not. A scheme with better results appears in [KY01].

2.2.3 Symmetrical Private Information Retrieval

Symmetrical PIR is a PIR problem, where the privacy of the database is considered. That is, a Symmetrical PIR protocol must prevent user from learning about more than one record of the database during a session. Clearly, symmetrical privacy (database privacy) would be required for practical applications, since only then is an efficient billing possible. Symmetrical PIR protocol for a single server was first considered in [KO97]; and for several servers it was considered in [GIKM98]. Other symmetrical PIR were later proposed in [Mis00, MS00, NP99a]. The protocols presented in the next three subsections satisfy the symmetrical PIR criteria as well.

2.2.4 Hardware-Based Private Information Retrieval

The protocol in [SS01] attains optimal communication complexity – $O(1)$ record per query (Figure 2.2). The protocol uses a secure coprocessor (SC)

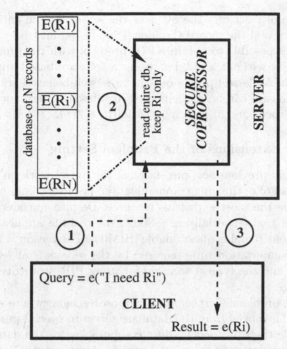

Fig. 2.2. An example of a PIR protocol with SC.

[Yee94, SPW98, DLP+01], a device installed on the server that can be briefly described as follows:

- The SC consists of a processor with some RAM and ROM all-over protected physically. No one can see the data processed inside the SC.
- There is software installed inside the SC. In particular, it may be software implementing a PIR protocol (see Figure 2.2).
- The SC generates a private/public key pair. The private key is kept inside the SC. The public key is available to everyone for securely communicating with the SC, without revealing the data to third parties, including the server.
- To any user the SC can always prove, which software is installed and whether it was changed in the past.

The idea of Smith et al. is to use a SC as a black box installed at the server site. The selection of the requested record takes place inside the SC. The basic protocol runs as shown in Figure 2.2. The client encrypts the query "return the i-th record" with a public key of the SC, and sends it to the SC via the server. The SC receives the encrypted query, decrypts it, and reads through the entire database (by interacting with the server), but but only leaves the requested record in memory. The protocol is finished after the SC encrypts the record with the user's key and sends it to the client. The server has no evidence of i because the SC asks the server for the entire database in order not to reveal the record the user is interested in.

Whether it is possible to obtain a PIR protocol with the same communication complexity without a SC, i.e., using a software-based approach only, is an open issue. Anderson points out that the well-believed statement "everything in hardware can be implemented in software" may not be the case with secure coprocessors, in principle ([And01], p.278).

2.2.5 Further Extensions of the Problem Setting

As can be seen in previous sections, most of the initial work on PIR has focused on the goal of optimizing communication, because communication was considered to be the most expensive resource. Despite considerable success in realizing this goal (especially in [SS00]), the real-life applicability of the proposed solutions remains questionable [BIM00]. The reason is that in most solutions, the computation time required by the servers is at least linear in database size[2]; and the typical scenario for using PIR protocols is when the database is large.

To solve this problem, Gertner et al. propose a scheme where most computation workload is moved from the database server to special purpose servers [GGM98]. While their protocols reduce computation for the database server to $O(1)$, the computation of the special-purpose servers is still linear for every query.

Di-Crescenzo et al. present another PIR scheme [CIO98] that utilizes special-purpose servers. In this model, most computation and communication is moved off-line (i.e., it is performed only once, independently from the number of further queries). Both in [CIO98] and in [GGM98] the user privacy is not protected if all servers cooperate against the user.

While Gertner et al. moved most computation to a more convenient place (special-purpose servers) [GGM98], Beimel et al. shifted most computation to a more convenient time (off-line). It is demonstrated that, while operating without any preprocessing linear computation is unavoidable, with preprocessing and some extra storage computation can be reduced. Namely, Beimel et al. have the following results for the Theoretical PIR and any $k \geq 2$ and $\epsilon > 0$:

1. A k-server protocol with $O(N^{1/(2k-1)})$ communication, $O(N/\epsilon log^{2k-2} N)$ work, and $O(N^{1+\epsilon})$ extra storage bits.
2. A k-server protocol with $O(N^{1/k+\epsilon})$ communication and work, and $O(N^{1+\epsilon})$ extra storage bits.

The ability to offer targeted web advertising without revealing user preferences (a problem similar to PIR) is investigated in [Jue01].

---

[2] The server has to read the entire database to answer one query. If the server-side protocol leaves one of the records unread, then the server can conclude that this record is not preferred by the user. This breaks the user privacy.

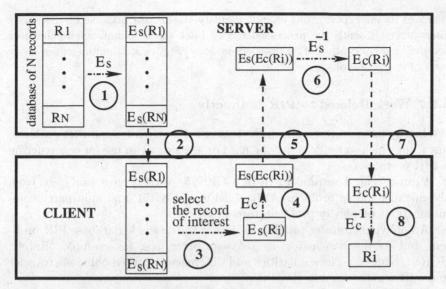

Fig. 2.3. An example of a PIR protocol with preprocessing and offline communication. Steps 1 and 2 are made offline once, and the other steps are performed online for every query submission.

Comparative Security Analysis of PIR. Relationships between different security primitives and the PIR problem are discussed in [CMO00, Man98, KO00, BIKM99, CY01]. We skip any further details on this subject because this does not relate to the work presented in this book.

2.2.6 PIR with Preprocessing and Offline Communication

Although it does not seem feasible to break the fundamental limitation - $O(N)$ I/Os to answer one query, one could try to reduce the $O(N)$ query response time. The idea is to let the database server preprocess as much work as possible, so that when a query is submitted it would cost only $O(1)$ I/Os to answer it online. This approach differs from the preprocessing approaches presented above in that it assumes no additional servers.

With this idea in mind, [BDF00, SJ00] independently present very similar PIR protocols. Both utilize homomorphic encryption, which is used by the server to encrypt every record of the database. All of these encrypted records are sent to the client. This communication has to be done only once between the client and the server when the PIR protocol starts, independently from how many PIR queries will be processed online.

If the user wants to query or to buy a record, he selects the appropriate (stored at the client) encrypted record and re-encrypts it. The user then sends it to the server and asks to remove the server's encryption. The server is able to do this because of the homomorphic property of the encryption. The server removes its encryption, but cannot identify the record because of the user's encryption. It sends the processed record back to the client, where the user removes his encryption. The protocol is done. Figure 2.3 demonstrates every step of the protocol.

2.2.7 Work Related to PIR Indirectly

We briefly mention research which does not directly solve the PIR problem, but from which some ideas may be used or are already in use for constructing a PIR protocol.

Protocols for Theoretical PIR in [CGKS95, Amb97] have used ideas from the instance hiding problem [AFK89, BF90, BFKR91] and multiparty communication complexity problem, respectively.

An oblivious transfer problem is similar to the single database PIR problem, but its research history is 15 years older (see, for example, [Rab81, BCR86, NP99b]). The similarities and differences between oblivious transfer and PIR are discussed in [CMO00].

The PIR problem can also be seen as a simple case of secure multiparty computations in general, and as a computing with encrypted function problem in particular. For example, the single database PIR protocol in [KO97] has the same basic idea as used in the scheme of computing with encrypted function introduced in [ST97]. A hardware-based PIR solution [SS00] is a particular case of secure multiparty computations based on secure coprocessors [Yee94].

Finally, for completeness reason we mention, that the earliest (to our best knowledge) record of a problem similar to PIR takes place in the 17-18th century[3]; the author is unknown.

2.3 Analysis of the Previous Approaches

In this section, we first agree on the exact evaluation criteria for PIR approaches. Next, we choose the best (state of the art) PIR solutions in terms of the evaluation criteria. In addition, we point out to the drawbacks of these solutions and shortly outline the structure of this book.

2.3.1 Evaluation Criteria for PIR Approaches

Naturally, PIR protocols are judged by query response time and by the amount of communication between the server and user required to execute a query.

---

[3] We refer the reader to the story "Go there, I won't tell you where; Bring me that, I won't tell you what" [Afa76].

Table 2.1. State of the art PIR Approaches.

Parameter	PIR Protocol	
	[SS00, SS01]	[BDF00, SJ00]
Communication (online)	optimal	optimal
Response time	$O(N)$	$O(1)$
Communication (offline)	no	$O(N)$
Preprocessing	no	yes

The lower bound of communication between the client and server should be comparable to the size of one record. The reason for this is that exactly one record is communicated from the server to the user while answering a "return the i-th record" query without any PIR.

The query response time depends on the number of database I/Os that the server must perform. For most PIR protocols proposed, the number of I/Os per query is $O(N)$, since the server must read the entire database before answering one query[4]. However, if no PIR is required, it takes only one record I/O (reading the i-th record of the array) to answer a "return the i-th record" query. From this we can conclude that the natural lower bound for query response time complexity for PIR is $O(1)$.

In case there is a preprocessing phase in a protocol in addition to the two mentioned criteria, two further criteria are considered: Communication complexity at preprocessing phase and the number of database I/Os that the server must perform for preprocessing.

2.3.2 State of the Art

The lower bound for communication complexity is reached by a single protocol in the related work – [SS00, SS01]. Indeed, $O(1)$ records are sent from the server to the user to answer one query. The main disadvantage of this protocol is the same as for all other PIR protocols without preprocessing (including [KO97, CMS99, KY01]): It is $O(N)$ query response time implied by the $O(N)$ complexity of the number of I/Os to answer one query (Table 2.1).

The lower bound for query response time is demonstrated by the approach presented in [BDF00, SJ00]. Using preprocessing and offline communication, these protocols bypass the fundamental limitation, and gain $O(1)$ query response time, i.e., only one record must be processed online to answer a query. However, the protocols suffer from another drawback: This is offline communication comparable to the size of the entire database that makes their practical applicability questionable. Imagine if a user decides to buy a single digital book or a music file. He will probably change his mind if asked to download the entire encrypted content of the digital store in order to proceed with the purchase. Another problem is keeping the client's database copy up to date.

---

[4] Recall that the server can observe the records uninteresting to the user whenever the server does not read the entire database to answer a query. Thus, some information about i is revealed, violating the user's privacy by definition.

2.3.3 Open Problems

After analyzing the PIR model (described in Section 1.1) and the state of the art PIR approaches (summarized in Section 2.3.2), we identify two general problems associated with PIR[5]. This book tackles (and updates the state of the art with new approaches for) both of them.

– One general problem is that the existing state of the art in PIR forces the user to decide between downloading the entire database or waiting $O(N)$ time for query response in order to execute a PIR query. Both alternatives are intolerable for large databases. Part II of this book improves the state of the art in PIR by approaching a solution that has both $O(1)$ communication and query response time complexities. Note that we stick to the conventional PIR model in this part.
– Another general problem associated with PIR is its unpretentious model, already discussed in Section 1.1. Part III generalizes the conventional (simple) PIR model to meet the real-world requirements.

---

[5] Our observations partially intersect with those given in future work section of a Ph.D. thesis of Tal Malkin [Mal00].

Part II

Almost Optimal PIR

3 PIR with $O(1)$ Query Response Time and $O(1)$ Communication

In Section 3.1 we introduce a basic version of the PIR protocol with $O(1)$ query response time and communication. Section 3.2 formally defines the privacy property of a PIR protocol. Based on the two previous sections and Shannon's information theory, we formally prove in Section 3.3 that the proposed protocol provides privacy property.

3.1 Basic Protocol

Before describing the protocol itself, we will compare our solution to the previously proposed state of the art PIR protocols. One protocol uses a secure coprocessor to provide optimal $O(1)$ communication complexity and $O(N)$ query response time [SS00, SS01]. Yet another set of protocols employs server preprocessing to reduce the response time complexity to $O(1)$ [BDF00, SJ00], but introduces $O(N)$ communication between the client and server (Table 3.1). Our protocol, described below, combines the properties of secure coprocessors with a novel preprocessing approach, attaining $O(1)$ query response time with an optimal $O(1)$ communication complexity. The protocol is almost optimal; the only parameter left to improve is the server's preprocessing complexity - the least critical one[1].

Table 3.1. State of the art and the proposed PIR protocol.

Parameter	PIR Protocol		
	[SS00, SS01]	[BDF00, SJ00]	This Chapter
online comm.	optimal	optimal	optimal
Response time	$O(N)$	$O(1)$	$O(1)$
offline comm.	no	$O(N)$	no
Preprocessing	no	yes	yes

We start with the same basic model as described in Section 2.2.4. However, as a preprocessing phase, the SC shuffles the records before starting the PIR

---

[1] Moreover, improving preprocessing complexity is the subject of the next Chapter.

D. Asonov: Querying Databases Privately, LNCS 3128, 23–35, 2004.
© Springer-Verlag Berlin Heidelberg 2004

protocol. That is, the SC computes a random permutation of all records, and stores this permutation in an encrypted form. The idea is to reveal no information to the server about which record is which in a shuffled database. Thus, the SC could access the required records without reading the entire database.

After the user sends the query "return the i-th record", the SC does not read the entire database. Instead, the SC only reads the desired encrypted record. Next, the encrypted record is decrypted inside the SC, encrypted with the user's key, and sent to the user. To answer this query, $O(1)$ computation and communication is necessary online, resulting in an $O(1)$ query response time complexity.

Assume that to answer a second query, the SC reads the requested record only. If the SC reads a different record from the one accessed by the first query, one concludes that the queries are different. If the SC reads the same record, then the queries are the same. In both cases some information about user queries is revealed. Even more information is revealed about one of the queries if the other one is issued by (and known to) the server itself.

Therefore, to reveal no information about user queries, the SC must read the previously accessed records first, and then the desired record. In case the second query requests the same record as the first query, the SC chooses some random record to read. We formally prove this strategy in Section 3.3. In particular, the latter case is discussed in Example 3.2.1 of Section 3.2.

We note that the number of records read in order to answer one query grows with the number of queries answered. Thus it is important to perform preprocessing periodically to prepare new shuffled databases. Therefore, the SC can switch to a new shuffled database when some threshold number of records read per query is reached.

Having introduced the underlying idea, we propose the preprocessing algorithm for the SC in Section 3.1.1, designed to to shuffle a database. The protocol for the SC and the users is presented in Section 3.1.2. The algorithm for the SC to process a query online is described in Section 3.1.3. The rest of Section 3.1 is accessory material. Namely, we show a trade-off between preprocessing workload and query response time, and discuss choosing the optimal trade-off in Sections 3.1.4 and 3.1.5 respectively. Finally, we briefly consider cases with multiple queries and multiple secure coprocessors. The general scheme is illustrated in Figure 3.1.

3.1.1 Database Shuffling Algorithm (SSA)

The purpose of a shuffling algorithm is to generate a random permutation of the database records ([Knu81], Section 3.4.2). However, the peculiarity of our shuffling algorithm is that the SC must not reveal the permutation index to anyone, not even to the server. We focus on building this specific algorithm, omitting how the permutation index itself is obtained inside the SC.

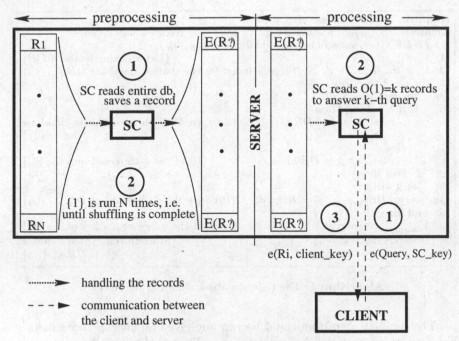

Fig. 3.1. I/O flows in the proposed PIR protocol.

To produce a shuffled database, the SC executes Algorithm 1[2]. Offline, the SC invokes a PIR protocol similar to the one described in Section 2.2.4 N times. With each of these invocations it privately reads one record that is chosen according to the permutation index. It then encrypts and writes this record to a new database. Having a permutation index V' to address these records, the SC can now access any encrypted record directly, without revealing the identity of the accessed record. The only operations observable from outside the SC are the *read* and *write* operations, which are used to access external storage.

The complexity of this algorithm is $O(N^2)$, since the SC reads N records to produce each of the N records in the shuffled database. This is because we assume herein that only a constant number of records can be stored simultaneously in the RAM of a SC[3]. Otherwise, if for instance all N records could be stored in a SC, the shuffling can be done with $O(N)$ complexity. In general, if the SC has enough memory to store $O(z)$ records, the shuffling complexity results in $O(N^2/z)$ I/Os.

---

[2] Herein we do not mention the page where an algorithm appears if it is on the same (or the next) page from where we are referring it.

[3] For Algorithm 1, we assume two records (*Temp*, *Record*) can be stored in the SC.

Require: DB: a database of N records
Ensure: $DB_{shuffled}$: a shuffled copy of DB, each record is encrypted;
    $INDEX_{shuffled}$: an encrypted index of $DB_{shuffled}$
1: $V = [1, ..., N]$ {Index of the database DB}
2: $V' = shuffle(V)$ {Prepare index for the shuffled database $DB_{shuffled}$}
3: **for** $g = 1$ to N **do**
4:    **for** $h = 1$ to N **do**
5:      **if** $h = V'[g]$ **then**
6:        $read(Record \Leftarrow DB[h])$ {Save the $V'[g]$-th record of the database
                                            internally}
7:      **else**
8:        $read(Temp \Leftarrow DB[h])$ {Read the h-th record into the SC}
9:      **end if**
10:   **end for**
11:   $write(DB_{shuffled}[g] \Leftarrow Record)$ {Produce the g-th record of $DB_{shuffled}$}
12: **end for**
13: $V'_{encrypted} = encrypt(V')$ {Encrypt the index with a key of the SC}
14: $write(INDEX_{shuffled} \Leftarrow V'_{encrypted})$ {Store the encrypted index of
                                                      $DB_{shuffled}$}

Algorithm 1: The basic database shuffling algorithm.

The shuffling algorithm could be run any given number of times beforehand, to produce several shuffled databases. The only limitation for a preprocessing algorithm is the quantity of additional storage available to the server. Therefore, Section 3.1.4 defines the preprocessing workload parameter as an average amount of additional storage (per query) used in preprocessing.

In the following chapters we will consider considerably more complex shuffling algorithms. This is why we call this algorithm the straightforward shuffling algorithm (SSA).

3.1.2 The Protocol

This subsection presents the protocol between the server and clients for processing queries. To answer the k-th query, the SC has to read $k-1$ previously read records first. It then reads one additional record. Evidently, the SC has to keep a track (T) of the accessed records.

As k grows, the query response time grows as well. It is up to the server to decide for which point $m = max(k)$ $(1 \leqslant m \leqslant N)$ to stop and to switch to another preprocessed (shuffled) copy of the database, so that k is equal to 1 again. Since m is a constant independent of N, the server has to perform $O(1)$ computations and I/Os to answer each query online.

The protocol refers to an algorithm required by a SC to process a query, which is described in the next section.

(1) The SC initializes a query counter $k = 1$, loads the index V' of a shuffled database into the internal memory, and initializes the track of accessed records $T = \{\varnothing\}$.

(2) The user comes up with a query $Q = $ "return the i-th record", or simply
    $Q = i$.
(3) The client and the SC generate and exchange symmetric keys Key_c and
    Key_{sc} using a public key infrastructure.
(4) The client sends the encrypted query $E(Q, Key_{sc})$ to the server.
(5) The SC receives and decrypts the query.
(6) The SC runs Algorithm 2 to get the answer $A = R_i{}^4$.
(7) The SC sends the encrypted answer $E(A, Key_c)$ to the client.
(8) The client decrypts the answer.
(9) The SC increments k by one.
    If $k > m$, the SC switches to a new shuffled database, reloads the
    corresponding index, re-initializes the query counter $k = 1$ and the
    track of accessed records $T = \{\varnothing\}$.
(10) To process another query, steps 2 through 9 are repeated.

3.1.3 An Algorithm for Processing a Query

Algorithm 2 is executed inside the SC, and is used as a part of the protocol. The only operations observable from outside the SC are *read* operations
for accessing the shuffled database. As discussed above, the complexity of
this algorithm is $O(1)$. The logic of this algorithm was discussed above in
Section 3.1.

3.1.4 Trade-Off between Preprocessing Workload
and Query Response Time

For our protocol it is possible to balance the workload between query processing and preprocessing. Decreasing the amount of online I/Os increases the
preprocessing work, and vice versa. As already introduced in Section 3.1.2,
let m $(1 \leqslant m \leqslant N)$ be a maximal number of records allowed to be read
online in response to a single query. Obviously, m is a trade-off parameter.
As we show in this section, reducing m will decrease the response time of the
server, but will increase the amount of preprocessing.

Let $\mathbf{r}_{online}$ be the average number of encrypted records that the SC reads
online to answer a query. This parameter characterizes the average response
time of the server. Let $\mathbf{w}_{offline}$ be the average number of encrypted records
that the SC writes during the preprocessing stage in order to be prepared
to answer one query. This parameter characterizes the average amount of
additional storage used by the SC for answering one query. Our equations
below express both parameters using the trade-off parameter.

$$\mathbf{r}_{online} = \frac{1 + 2 + 3 + \dots + m}{m} = \frac{m+1}{2} \tag{3.1}$$

---

[4] Algorithm 2 uses i, V', and T to privately retrieve the requested record into the
SC; it also updates T appropriately.

Require: $DB_{shuffled}, V'$: a shuffled copy of DB (each record is encrypted) and
its index;
   k: the sequence number of the query being processed using $DB_{shuffled}$;
   i: the number of the DB record requested
Ensure: *Answer*: record R_i of DB privately retrieved into the SC

1: $g = 1$; *GotAnswer = No*
2: **while** $g < k$ **do**
3:    $read(Temp \Leftarrow DB_{shuffled}[T[g]])$ {Read previously accessed records one by
                                                                                    one}
4:    **if** $V'[T[g]] = i$ **then**
5:       $Answer = Temp$ {One of the accessed records is the answer, save it}
6:       $GotAnswer = Yes$
7:    **end if**
8:    $g = g + 1$
9: **end while**
10: **if** *GotAnswer = No* **then**
11:    $obtain \ i' : V'[i'] = i$ {Get the position of the i-th DB record in $DB_{shuffled}$}
12:    $read(Answer \Leftarrow DB_{shuffled}[i'])$ {Access the required record directly}
13:    $T[k] = i'$ {The track list is updated with the k-th item}
14: **else**
15:    $UnRead = \{1, ... N\} \setminus \{T[1], ..., T[k-1]\}$
16:    $h = select\_random\_from(UnRead)$ {Randomly select one of the unread
                                                                                    records}
17:    $read(Temp \Leftarrow DB_{shuffled}[h])$ {Read the selected record into the SC}
18:    $T[k] = h$ {The track list is updated with the k-th item}
19: **end if**
20: **return** *Answer*

Algorithm 2: An algorithm for processing k-th query.

$$\mathbf{w}_{offline} = \frac{N}{m} \tag{3.2}$$

The dependencies between the trade-off parameter m, the online work $\mathbf{r}_{online}$,
and the preprocessing parameter $\mathbf{w}_{offline}$ are shown in Figure 3.2 (for $N = 10000$).

   From equations 3.1 and 3.2 we derive the dependence between the processing ($\mathbf{r}_{online}$) and preprocessing ($\mathbf{w}_{offline}$) parameters of the protocol.

$$\mathbf{r}_{online} = \frac{N}{2 \cdot \mathbf{w}_{offline}} + 1 = \Theta\left(\frac{N}{\mathbf{w}_{offline}}\right) \tag{3.3}$$

The last equation exhibits each reduction of the query response time by an
order leading to an increase in preprocessing work by an order.

3.1.5 Choosing the Optimal Trade-Off

One could easily determine the trade-off parameter m given the limit for the
query response time of the server.

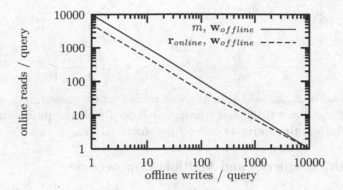

Fig. 3.2. The dependence between query response time (max and average number of records to read online per query) and preprocessing workload (number of offline write operations per query).

Another strategy for choosing the trade-off parameter might be minimizing the overall work $S(m)$, defined as the sum of the normalized processing and preprocessing workload parameters:

$$S(m) = \mathbf{r}_{online} \cdot \varphi_{norm} + \mathbf{w}_{offline} \qquad (3.4)$$

where φ_{norm} is the normalization coefficient used to normalize the two parameters.

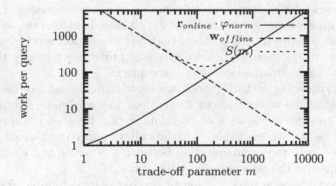

Fig. 3.3. The overall work done per query (calculated as a sum of normalized processing and preprocessing parameters) is not constant for different values of the trade-off parameter.

In Figure 3.3 we show that the overall work $S(m)$ does not remain constant while varying the trade-off parameter. We resolve the optimal trade-off by finding the roots of the derivative of $S(m)$:

$$S'(m) = \left(\frac{(m+1) \cdot \varphi_{norm}}{2} + \frac{N}{m}\right)' = \frac{\varphi_{norm}}{2} - \frac{N}{m^2};$$

$$\frac{\varphi_{norm}}{2} - \frac{N}{m_{opt}^2} = 0, \qquad m_{opt} = \left\lceil \sqrt{\frac{2 \cdot N}{\varphi_{norm}}} \right\rceil \qquad (3.5)$$

For example, if $\varphi_{norm} = 1$ (reading one record while answering a query is considered equal to writing and storing one record while preprocessing), and $N = 10000$, then the optimal trade-off parameter is $m_{opt} = \lceil \sqrt{2 \cdot N} \rceil = 141$.

3.1.6 Multiple Queries and Multiple Coprocessors

Multi-query optimization may be advantageous for our protocol. When several queries arrive at the server, the SC may read previously accessed records only once, thus eliminating the need to perform this operation for every query[5].

Splitting the workload across several SCs is an easy task. For example, due to little online workload, one SC might be dedicated to answering queries; and the rest of the secure coprocessors can do the preprocessing work, i.e. preparing several shuffled copies of the database. Such a simple parallelization is possible since preprocessing can be done independently from query processing.

3.2 Formal Definition of the Privacy Property

The protocol in [SS00] reveals no information about user queries: The only observable information is that the SC reads all records to answer each query. It is not that obvious for our protocol that no information is revealed about user queries. In the next section we formally prove the property that our protocol reveals no information about user queries.

Before proceeding with the proof, we must formally capture the notion "no information about user queries is revealed" in mathematical terms. Definitions in previous work, such as "communication between the server and client must be indistinguishable", are difficult to apply in this case. In our protocol, not only the communication between the server and client is observable, but so is the preprocessing work of the SC.

We exploit Shannon's information theory to use its definition of information measure [Sha48]. It is essential for the presentation that we first give a sketch of how the amount of information is formally measured using information theory. In case the reader has a general understanding of information theory, we advise skipping the next section and proceeding to the privacy definition presented in Section 3.2.2.

---

[5] Note that the detailed picture for multi-query processing may look more complicated. We have only sketched the basic idea above.

3.2.1 Basics of Information Theory

Informally, the information known about a variable i is defined as a predictability of this variable [Jay94]. The measure of predictability is defined using the measure of unpredictability (entropy) - the central notion in Shannon's theory. Formally defining entropy is one of the main goals of the theory. The way this goal is achieved is briefly explained below. During the preparation of this short survey, several sources were used, including [Sha48, Jay94, Mac00, Sch96].

Let X be a random variable, and let A_X be the set of values this variable may take. Let the number of elements of the set A_X be N. Finally, by x_j we denote the j-th element of A_X, $x_j \in A_X$. A random variable X is presented as a vector of probabilities $X = < P(x_1), ..., P(x_N) >$. Similarly, $Y = < P(y_1), ..., P(y_N) >$.

The amount of information known about variable X is measured by the entropy of this variable $H(X)$. Informally, the entropy is a measure of the "uncertainty" of X. If the entropy is zero, one knows the exact value of the variable – as shown in Equation 3.7 below. If the entropy is maximal for this variable, one knows nothing about this variable except its size – as shown in Equation 3.8 below.

The entropy is defined as a function H with the following properties:

1. H should be continuous in the $P(x_j)$. Otherwise an arbitrary small change in the probability distribution would still lead to the same big change in the amount of uncertainty.
2. This function should correspond qualitatively to common sense, in that when there are many possibilities we are more uncertain than when there are few. This condition implies that, for $P(x_i)$ being all equal, the quantity

$$h(N) = H\left(\frac{1}{N}, ..., \frac{1}{N}\right)$$

   is a monotonically increasing function of N.
3. Informally, the measure H should be consistent, i.e., if there is more than one way of working out its value, the answers must be the same. Formally, if a choice is broken down into two successive choices, the original value of H should be the weighted sum of the values of H for individual choices. Figure 3.4 provides an example. For this special case, we require that

$$H(0.6, 0.32, 0.08) = H(0.6, 0.4) + 0.4 \cdot H(0.8, 0.2).$$

The coefficient 0.4 is the weighting factor.

Shannon's Theorem proves that the only function satisfying the given properties is the following one (a multiplicative constant is usually omitted):

$$H(X) = \sum_{x \in A_X} P(x) \cdot log \frac{1}{P(x)} \tag{3.6}$$

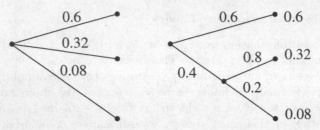

Fig. 3.4. Decomposition of a choice from three possibilities.

With the definition of entropy, one can prove the following properties:

$$H(X) \geqslant 0 \quad \text{with equality iff} \qquad (3.7)$$
$$P(x_j) = 1 \quad \text{for one } j \in 1, ..., N.$$
$$H(X) \leqslant \log N \quad \text{with equality iff} \qquad (3.8)$$
$$P(x_j) = 1/N \text{ for all } j \in 1, ..., N.$$

The joint entropy, i.e., the entropy of a set of variables is calculated by:

$$H(X,Y) = \sum_{xy \in A_X A_Y} P(x,y) \cdot \log \frac{1}{P(x,y)} \qquad (3.9)$$

In case of variable independence, the joint entropy is calculated as a sum of the entropies of the variables:

$$H(X,Y) = H(X) + H(Y) \text{ if } P(x,y) = P(x) \cdot P(y) \qquad (3.10)$$

The joint entropy of a set of variables has the same meaning as the entropy of a variable. That is, no information about a set of variables is revealed iff the joint entropy is maximal.

It can be shown that the joint entropy $II(X,Y)$ is maximal iff

$$H(X) = H(Y) = logN, \; P(x,y) = P(x) \cdot P(y) \qquad (3.11)$$

Then the maximal entropy is due to (3.10) and (3.11):

$$H(X,Y) = H_{max}(X) + H_{max}(Y) = 2 \cdot logN$$

In summary, we say that no information is revealed if the corresponding entropy is maximal. In particular, no information is revealed about a set of variables if the joint entropy of these variables is maximal. The joint entropy may only reach its maximum for independent variables, and, in this case, it can be calculated by the sum of the entropies of the variables.

3.2.2 Privacy Definition

Based on the introduction to information theory, we define the privacy property of a protocol as the absence of information about a set of processed queries $Q_1, ..., Q_k$ (and their results). Due to the information theory, there is no information revealed about the set of variables $Q_1, ..., Qk$ if and only if the joint entropy $H(Q_1, ..., Q_k)$ of these variables is maximal.

Definition 3.2.1 (Privacy Property of a Protocol). *Assume that queries* $Q_1, ..., Q_k$ *are processed using a given protocol. This protocol is private (i.e. this protocol attains privacy property) iff the joint entropy of variables* $Q_1, ..., Q_k$ *is maximal.*

We offer the following example to demonstrate the definition.

Example 3.2.1 (Calculating the Joint Entropy). We consider two queries, Q_1 and Q_2. Each of these queries is presented as a variable equal to a number from 1 to N, meaning the number of the record being retrieved. We consider two cases. First case: the observer has no information about the set of variables Q_1, Q_2. Second case: the observer has no information about variables, except the fact that $Q_1 = Q_2$.

Intuitively, half of the information about the set of two variables is revealed in the second case. After calculating the joint entropies for both cases, we check if the joint entropies correlate in the same way.

To calculate joint entropies we need the individual entropies $H(Q_1)$ and $H(Q_2)$. The individual entropies $H(Q_1)$ and $H(Q_2)$ are calculated with (3.6, Section 3.2.1), using the corresponding probabilities:

$$P(Q_1 = 1) = P(Q_1 = 2) = ... = P(Q_1 = N) = \frac{1}{N},$$

$$P(Q_2 = 1) = P(Q_2 = 2) = ... = P(Q_2 = N) = \frac{1}{N}.$$

In both cases the individual entropies $H(Q_1)$ and $H(Q_2)$ are maximal (3.6,3.8):

$$H(Q_1) = \sum_{1 \leq j \leq N} P(Q_1 = j) \cdot log \frac{1}{P(Q_1 = j)} = H(Q_2) = logN$$

In the first case, the joint entropy is calculated as the sum of the individual entropies (3.10):

$$H(Q_1, Q_2) = H(Q_1) + H(Q_2) = logN + logN = 2 \cdot logN$$

In the second case, the joint entropy is calculated due to (3.9) for $1 \leq j \leq N, 1 \leq k \leq N$:

$$H(Q_1, Q_2 \equiv Q_1) = \sum_{j,k} P(Q_1 = j, Q_2 = k) \cdot log \frac{1}{P(Q_1 = j, Q_2 = k)} =$$

$$\sum_j P(Q_1 = j, Q_2 = j) \cdot log \frac{1}{P(Q_1 = j, Q_2 = j)} =$$

$$\sum_{1 \leq j \leq N} P(Q_1 = j) \cdot log \frac{1}{P(Q_1 = j)} = logN$$

The last two equations demonstrate the correspondence between the notion of entropy and our intuition in that the entropy of two unknown independent variables is twice as large as the entropy of two unknown equal variables. □

3.3 Proof of the Privacy Property of the Protocol

Based on the definition of the privacy property (Section 3.2, Definition 3.2.1) and on the formal description of the protocol (Section 3.1), we formally prove that our protocol has the privacy property.

Theorem 3.3.1 (The proposed protocol is private). *The protocol proposed in Section 3.1 attains privacy property (as defined by Definition 3.2.1).*

Proof. Let S be a set of queries $Q_1, ... Q_k$ (for any k) executed so far using the protocol. Due to the definition of privacy (Section 3.2), we have to prove that, for any observer, e.g. the server, the joint entropy of the set of queries $Q_1, ... Q_k$ is maximal:

$$H(Q_1, ..., Q_k) = k \cdot logN \tag{3.12}$$

To prove (3.12), it is sufficient (3.11) to prove two claims:

1. The queries are independent for an observer:

$$P(Q_1, ..., Q_k) = P(Q_1) \cdot P(Q_2) \cdot ... \cdot P(Q_k)$$

2. The entropy of each query is maximal:

$$H(Q_1) = H(Q_2) = ... = H(Q_k) = logN$$

We prove both claims by induction. First, we consider the number of queries $k = 1$. Second, we also consider the case of $k = 2$. Third, we assume that the claims are true for $k = K$ and prove the same for $k = K + 1$.

For $k = 1$, only one query Q_1 is processed after the database was shuffled with Algorithm 1. Due to Algorithm 2, the SC directly reads the required encrypted record to answer the query. The first claim is obviously true because the set of answered queries contains only one query. Since the records were randomly permutated with the shuffling algorithm, reading the encrypted record reveals no correspondence to the original record. This proves the second claim to be true too:

$$P(Q_1 = 1) = ... = P(Q_1 = N) = \frac{1}{N}; \quad H(Q_1) = H_{max}(Q_1) = logN$$

Consider the case $k = 2$. Due to the protocol, the server answers the second query after reading the previously accessed record and one of the unread records from the shuffled database. Since the server reads one of the unread records independently from whether $Q_1 = Q_2$ or not (Lines 16 and 12 of Algorithm 2 respectively), Q_1 and Q_2 are independent variables for the observer. This proves the first claim to be true. Since the database is shuffled, Q_2 may be any number from 1 to N with equal probabilities. This proves the second claim to be also true.

$$P(Q_1, Q_2) = P(Q_1) \cdot P(Q_2); \quad H(Q_1) = H(Q_2) = logN$$

We assume that the claims are true for $k = K$, i.e.,

$$P(Q_1, ..., Q_K) = P(Q_1) \cdot ... \cdot P(Q_K); \quad H(Q_1) = ... = H(Q_K) = logN$$

We consider the execution of the $k = (K+1)$-th query with Algorithm 2. Since the SC reads all K previously read records plus one, there is no relationship between the new query and the previous ones. Taking the last equation into account, we have:

$$P(Q_1, ..., Q_K, Q_{K+1}) = P(Q_1) \cdot ... \cdot P(Q_K) \cdot P(Q_{K+1})$$

Similarly, since the SC accesses a shuffled database, Q_{K+1} could be of any value with equal probability for the observer.

$$H(Q_1) = ... = H(Q_K) = H(Q_{K+1}) = logN$$

The proof by induction is complete.   □

3.4 Summary

Existing PIR protocols either incur intolerable query response time (linear in the size of the database) or introduce offline communication (between the user and the server) proportional to the size of the entire database. Thus, it is infeasible to use these protocols for large databases.

We presented a new PIR protocol with preprocessing that has $O(1)$ response time and optimal communication complexity. This property is due to new periodical preprocessing based on shuffling, and is also due to the use of a secure coprocessor. Furthermore, we formally proved that our protocol reveals no information about user queries. We based our proof on the Shannon's Theory of Information.

In the next chapter we improve our protocol, in particular by designing a shuffling algorithm of a lower complexity.

4 Improving Processing and Preprocessing Complexity

Section 4.1 tunes the PIR protocol proposed in the previous chapter by reducing its query response time. Section 4.2 tunes the same PIR protocol by reducing shuffling (preprocessing) complexity. This problem appears to be considerably more complex than the one in Section 4.1. Thus Section 4.2 presents theoretical results only. The experimental results form the nucleus of Chapter 5.

In Sections 4.1 and 4.2, the approaches improve different characteristics of the PIR protocol (query response time or preprocessing complexity). In order to compare the effectiveness of these approaches with each other, we propose a single combined criteria to evaluate them in Section 4.3.

4.1 Decreasing Query Response Time

According to our protocol, k records must be read from the shuffled database in order to answer a query online, where k is the number of queries answered using the same shuffled copy of a database. Here we present an approach to keep the query response time independent from k by employing preprocessing online. The basic idea is to apply our protocol recursively [AS02].

After answering the k-th query, we propose shuffling all the previously read records. The shuffled database would then consist of the group of previously unread records and the group of previously read records, now newly shuffled. Reading one record from each of the two groups would be enough to answer a query privately. If the "reshuffling" of the previously accessed records takes place after each query, the query response time remains determined by 2 I/Os, and is independent of k.

Periodical switching to a new shuffled database is inevitable however, because the complexity of online shuffling of the previously accessed records grows with the number of queries answered, possibly resulting in delays for processing the following queries.

This unsophisticated approach only improves the query response time, providing no insights into how the shuffling (preprocessing) complexity could be decreased. In the next section we propose two approaches to decrease the preprocessing complexity.

D. Asonov: Querying Databases Privately, LNCS 3128, 37–47, 2004.
© Springer-Verlag Berlin Heidelberg 2004

4.2 Decreasing the Complexity of Shuffling

In this section we describe two independent techniques that decrease the pre-processing work. First, we design a shuffling algorithm with $O(N\sqrt{N})$ complexity compared to the $O(N^2)$ straightforward shuffling algorithm (SSA) proposed in Chapter 3. Second, we show how to recycle used shuffled databases as another way to reduce the work required for producing a new shuffled database.

4.2.1 Split-Shuffle-Gather Algorithm (SSG)

The shuffled database used in the protocol must be periodically substituted with a new one, in order to keep the query response time under a given threshold. The straightforward shuffling algorithm (SSA) introduced in Section 3.1.1 possesses $O(N^2)$ I/O complexity, which is rather heavy for an algorithm that must be executed periodically. This subsection introduces a novel shuffling algorithm with improved complexity (named SSG).

We present a preprocessing algorithm with $O(N^2/p)$ complexity for a SC (for any $p \leq L$) and $O(pN)$ complexity for an untrusted computer (UC)[1]. Furthermore, we show the optimal complexity for a SC together with a UC to be $O(\sqrt{N}N)$ (for $p = \sqrt{N}$), in contrast to the $O(N^2)$ complexity of the straightforward shuffling algorithm (SSA) proposed in Chapter 3.

The basic idea of the SSG algorithm is to (i) derive p smaller databases from the original one, (ii) shuffle each of the p databases using the same permutation vector, and (iii) gather the shuffled databases into a single shuffled database. Algorithm 3 formalizes the SSG algorithm while referring to three sub-algorithms that are explained in the following paragraphs.

Algorithm 4 splits each record of the database $DB[N]$ into p equal parts. For example, the database $DB_1[N]$ would consist of the first parts of the records of the original database; each record of the database $DB_1[N]$ would be of size L/p. Obviously, there would be p such databases $(DB_1[N], ..., DB_p[N])$. No SC is needed to perform this algorithm because it can be performed by an untrusted computer (UC). Figure 4.1(b) shows the output of this algorithm for $p = 2$.

Using Algorithm 5, the SC shuffles all of the databases using the same shuffling vector $(DB_1 \rightarrow DB_1^{shuffl}, DB_2 \rightarrow DB_2^{shuffl}, ..., DB_p \rightarrow DB_p^{shuffl})$, one by one. Shuffling a small database takes $(N/p)^2$ I/Os for the SC, because the SC reads p sequential records into its memory at a time. This results in $p * (N/p)^2$ sequential reads of blocks of size L to shuffle p small databases. Figure 4.1(c) shows an example of an output of this algorithm, for the input of Figure 4.1(b).

---

[1] By UC we mean any general purpose computational resource without tamper resistance. For example, the server is an untrusted computer.

Require: $DB[N]$: a database of N records of size L; a parameter p
Ensure: a shuffled copy of $DB[N]$, each record is encrypted; $INDEX_{shuffl}$: an
encrypted shuffling index
1: **if** Algorithm 4 has never been executed before **then**
2:    $execute(Algorithm\ 4)$ {Split the records of the database in p parts; j-th
part of each record is saved in $DB_j[N]$, $\forall j, 1 \le j \le p$}
3: **end if**
4: $execute(Algorithm\ 5)$ {Shuffle the p databases using the SC:
$DB_j \to DB_j^{shuffl}$ }
5: $execute(Algorithm\ 6)$ {Assemble the shuffled records of the original database
from their pieces}

Algorithm 3: The main preprocessing algorithm.

Require: $DB[N]$: a database of N records of size L; split factor p
Ensure: $\{DB_j[N]\}, j \in \{1,...,p\}$: p databases; an x-th record from the y-th
database $(DB_y[x])$ is the y-th part of $DB[x]$
1: **for** $h = 1$ to N **do**
2:    **for** $g = 1$ to p **do**
3:       $read(Temp \Leftarrow DB[h][g])$ {Read the g-th part of h-th record}
4:       $write(DB_g[h] \Leftarrow Temp)$ {Produce the h-th record of DB_g}
5:    **end for**
6: **end for**

Algorithm 4: The algorithm for splitting the database.

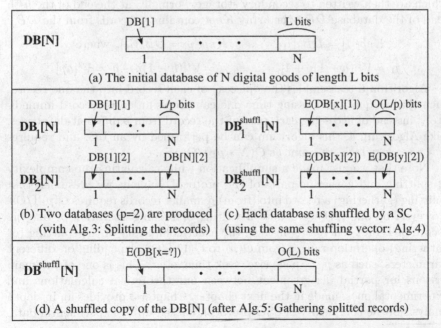

(a) The initial database of N digital goods of length L bits

(b) Two databases (p=2) are produced
(with Alg.3: Splitting the records)

(c) Each database is shuffled by a SC
(using the same shuffling vector: Alg.4)

(d) A shuffled copy of the DB[N] (after Alg.5: Gathering splitted records)

Fig. 4.1. An example of the preprocessing algorithm for $p = 2$.

Require: Output from Algorithm 4: $\{DB_j[N]\}, j \in \{1, ..., p\}$: p databases, each has N records of size L/p;
Ensure: $\{DB_j^{shuffl}[N]\}, j \in \{1, ..., p\}$: p shuffled databases;
   $INDEX_{shuffl}$: an encrypted shuffling index, the same for all split databases
1: $V = [1, ..., N]$; $V' = shuffle(V)$ {Use the same index to shuffle databases}
2: **for** $g = 1$ to p **do**
3:    **for** $h = 1$ to N/p **do**
4:       **for** $u = 1$ to N/p **do**
5:          $read\_into\_SC(Temp \Leftarrow DB_g[(u-1)p+1, ..., (u-1)p+p])$ {Read p
                                                                     sequential records of size L/p from DB_g}
6:          $map(Kept \Leftarrow Temp)$ {Fill positions in $Kept$ in accordance with V'}
7:       **end for**
8:       $write\_from\_SC(DB_g^{shuffl}[(h-1)*p+1, ..., (h-1)*p+1] \Leftarrow encrypt(Kept))$
                          {Produce p sequential records of size L/p for DB_g^{shuffl}, encrypt
                                                                                          separately}
9:    **end for**
10: **end for**
11: $V'_{encrypted} = encrypt(V')$ {Encrypt the index with some key of the SC}
12: $write\_from\_SC(INDEX_{shuffl} \Leftarrow V'_{encrypt})$ {The encrypted shuffling index}

Algorithm 5: The algorithm for shuffling the split databases.

Function map used in Algorithm 5 ensures that after each read of a database p (random) records remain in the memory of the SC (array $Kept$) which are then written to secondary storage. Formally, at the end of the h-th read of the database DB_g, the array $Kept$ contains p records from the DB_g:

$$Kept[1] = DB_g[j_1], \quad ... \quad , Kept[p] = DB_g[j_p], \text{ where}$$

$$j_1 = V'[(h-1)p+1], \quad ... \quad , j_p = V'[(h-1)p+p] = V'[hp]$$

Algorithm 6 reassembles the "pieces" of each record into the one record, such that at query processing time one can access an entire record immediately, instead of accessing each part of the record from p different databases. Like Algorithm 4, this algorithm can be performed by an UC, and requires $N * p$ reads, which we count as $O(N * p)$ I/Os.

Note that we just made a simplification while calculating the complexity of splitting and gathering parts of the protocol. Namely, we presumed that splitting (gathering) a record into (from) p smaller records requires $O(p)$ I/Os. However, by one I/O we denote a writing or reading operation of one big record of L bits. Therefore, in fact, the exact complexity of the splitting (or gathering) operation ranges from $O(p)$ to $O(1)$ I/Os, depending on different parameters, such as p, L, page size, seek time, etc.[2]. This is one of the main reasons for partial disagreement between our theoretical calculations and experimental ones, made in the next chapter. Chapter 5 provides an in-depth analysis of the complexity of SSG protocol, backed up by experimental data.

---
[2] For example, the complexity of splitting a record approaches $O(1)$ if p is rather small and L is large. Similarly, the complexity approaches $O(p)$ if p is large and L is small.

Require: Output from Algorithm 5: $\{DB_j^{shuffl}[N]\}, j \in \{1, ..., p\}$: p shuffled databases; the shuffling vector V' is the same for all databases
Ensure: $DB^{shuffl}[N]$: a shuffled copy of $DB[N]$; each record is encrypted
1: **for** $h = 1$ to N **do**
2:    **for** $g = 1$ to p **do**
3:       $read(Temp \Leftarrow DB_g^{shuffl}[h])$ {Read the g-th part of h-th record for DB_{shuffl}}
4:       $write(DB_g[h] \Leftarrow Temp)$ {Produce the g-th part for h-th record for DB_{shuffl}}
5:    **end for**
6: **end for**

Algorithm 6: The algorithm for assembling the shuffled database.

With the simplification mentioned above, the overall complexity of Algorithms 5 and 6 is $O(N^2/p + N * p)$. Namely, $O(N^2/p)$ is the complexity of the SC work, and $O(N * p)$ complexity is due to the work performed by an UC.

In the following subsection we determine the minimal complexity by varying parameter p.

4.2.2 Balancing the Preprocessing Complexity between SC and UC

In this subsection we study into how many pieces to split the initial database records, in order to gain optimal (i.e. minimal) complexity of the preprocessing algorithm (Algorithm 3).

Theorem 4.2.1. *The minimal complexity of Algorithm 3 is attained for $p = \sqrt{N}$.*

Proof. As follows from Section 4.2.1, the complexity of the preprocessing algorithm can be estimated by $O(N * p + N^2/p)$, given that the parameter $1 \leq p \leq L$ of the algorithm is specified.

To find the optimal p, we determine the minimum of the function $f(p) = N * p + N^2/p$.

$$f'(p) = (N * p + \frac{N^2}{p})' = N - \frac{N^2}{p^2}; \quad p_{opt} = \sqrt{N}.$$

Consequently, the optimal preprocessing complexity is:

$$O(f(p_{opt})) = O(2N\sqrt{N}) = O(N\sqrt{N})$$

This is also demonstrated in Fig 4.2 for $N = 10000$.   □

The above result for an optimal p is valid if $\sqrt{N} \leq L$, which is a rather reasonable assumption. Otherwise, if $\sqrt{N} > L$, the parameter should be assigned to the largest possible number, i.e. $p = L$.

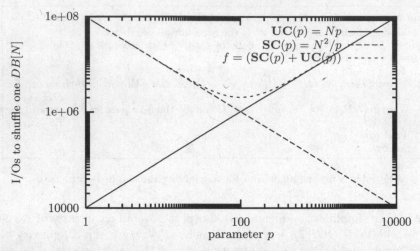

Fig. 4.2. The overall work done to shuffle one database (calculated as a sum of the number of I/Os for SC and UC) is not constant for different values of p.

The complexity of the work for the SC can be further reduced to $O(N)$ while at the same time leading to growth of the same order in the complexity of the work done by an UC, as shown in Figure 4.3.

4.2.3 Recycling Used Shuffled Databases

Due to our PIR protocol, the SC switches to a new shuffled database after answering m queries, in order to keep the query response time from growing above the $O(m)$ threshold. However, after answering $m < N$ queries, not all information about the records in the shuffled database is revealed. This can be interpreted as the SC not using the shuffled database "completely" [AF02b, AC02]. Instead, it stops using this database and starts using a new one. In this subsection we sketch an approach towards recycling a used database to produce a new shuffled database.

We propose to recycle the databases that cannot be used anymore for query processing. The recycling may be of less complexity than producing a shuffled copy of the database from scratch. Assume the SC has answered m queries before switching to a newly shuffled database. This means, the identities of m records must be presumed to be revealed. Consequently, the identities of $N-m$ records remain unknown. We restore the shuffled database using these $N-m$ records as a foundation. Formally, Algorithm 7 picks one of the known records and the $N-m$ shuffled records and produces $N-m+1$ shuffled records using $O(N-m+1)$ I/Os. The SC builds a completely shuffled database by iterating this algorithm m times.

We calculate the complexity C^{rec} for this "recycling" approach. Each of the items in the equation below corresponds to the complexity of each of the m iterations of Algorithm 7:

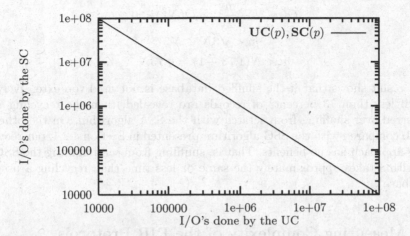

Fig. 4.3. At preprocessing, reducing the complexity of the SC results in the growth of the complexity of the UC and vice versa.

Require: $j - 1$ shuffled encrypted records $DB^{shuffl}[1, ..., j - 1]$; a record R
Ensure: $DB^{shuffl}[1, ..., j]$: j shuffled encrypted records; the newly added record R can be at any position.
1: $read\_into\_SC(Buf \Leftarrow R)$ {Read the record R into the SC}
2: **for** $g = 1$ to $j - 1$ **do**
3:     $read\_into\_SC(Temp \Leftarrow decrypt(DB^{shuffl}[g]))$ {Read the g-th record from
                                              DB_{shuffl}, decrypt it}
4:     $ifswap(Temp, Buf)$ {Swap the arguments or wait a given time to pretend to
                                              be swapping}
5:     $write\_from\_SC(DB^{shuffl}[g] \Leftarrow encrypt(Temp))$ {Write down the new g-th
                                              record for DB_{shuffl}}
6: **end for**
7: $write\_from\_SC(DB^{shuffl}[j] \Leftarrow encrypt(Buf))$ {Write down the record from
                                              the buffer of the SC}

Algorithm 7: The iterative shuffling algorithm for recycling a used shuffled database.

$$C^{rec}(N, m) = O(N - m + 1) + O(N - m + 2) + ... + O(N) =$$
$$O(N) + O(N) + ...O(N) + O(1) + O(2) + ... + O(m) =$$
$$O(mN) + O(\frac{m^2}{2}) = O(m(N + \frac{m}{2}))$$

The recycling only makes sense if its complexity is less than the complexity of shuffling from scratch. The complexity of the proposed recycling is less than shuffling a database from scratch using the SSA algorithm of $O(N^2)$ complexity, for all $m < 0.73N$:

$$O(m(N + \frac{m}{2})) - O(N^2) < 0$$
$$m < \sqrt{3}N - N$$
$$m < N(1.73 - 1) = 0.73N$$

This result shows that if the shuffled database is not used too extensively, i.e., if less than 73 percent[3] of records are revealed, then the recycling is preferred over shuffling from scratch with the SSA algorithm. On the other hand, compared with the SSG algorithm presented in Section 4.2.1, our recycling approach has no benefits. That is, shuffling from scratch using the SSG algorithm takes approximately the same or less time than recycling a used database[4].

4.3 Measuring Complexity of the PIR Protocols

We proposed several techniques for improving query processing and preprocessing parts of the almost optimal PIR protocol above. In this section, we measure how these improvements influence the overall complexity of the protocol when compared to each other. In order to be able to do this, we must first define a normalized complexity of a PIR protocol as follows.

4.3.1 A Normalized Measure for the Protocol Complexity

PIR protocols can be distinguished based on their preprocessing complexities and processing complexities. For example, the almost optimal protocol proposed in Chapter 3 preprocesses $P^{prep} = O(N^2/m)$ records per query, while exhibiting $P^{proc} = O(m)$ processing complexity. In the next subsection we compare, for example, this protocol to another one with different complexities of preprocessing and query response time. We define a single value measure for comparing the PIR protocols below.

Let us fix the query response time of a PIR protocol to $O(m)$. We then define the normalized complexity P of a PIR protocol by the complexity of the preprocessing work done per query. Our definition of the normalized complexity does not take into account the communication complexity of the protocol, because we only consider the protocols with optimal communication.

For a better understanding of the measurement, assume two PIR protocols. We adjust their processing complexities in such a way that they both exhibit a query response time $O(m)$. Now, the only difference in performance between them is how much time each of them have spent on preprocessing

---

[3] Please note that all calculations are done in $O()$, thus 73 is a very approximate number.

[4] The recycling algorithm can also be built based on the SSG algorithm to provide better recycling complexity. However, consideration of this case lies too far from the main goals of this book.

each answered query. That is, we assume that during the processing phase the same amount of work is done. The protocols can then be differentiated by how much preprocessing work per query is required.

4.3.2 The Measurement

In this section we measure and compare the normalized complexities of (i) the PIR protocol described in Chapter 3, (ii) the same protocol with improved preprocessing (SSG vs. SSA algorithm) as proposed in Section 4.2.1, (iii) the same protocol with improved query response time as proposed in Section 4.1. Finally, we consider the combination of both improvements and draw conclusions.

1. The protocol presented in Chapter 3 requires a preprocessing of complexity N^2 to be done in order to answer each m queries, providing the following normalized complexity:

$$P_1 = \frac{N^2}{m}$$

2. The protocol updated as proposed in Section 4.2.1 requires the preprocessing of complexity $N\sqrt{N}$ to be done in order to answer each m queries:

$$P_2 = \frac{N\sqrt{N}}{m}$$

3. The protocol updated as proposed in Section 4.1 has the same processing complexity in the worst case as the base protocol (Chapter 3). However, the idea explained in Section 4.1 can be applied to regenerating a used shuffled database. That is, after the m queries are executed, the shuffled database is not deleted. Instead, the accessed m records could be reshuffled, providing a shuffled database able to serve additional $m/2$ queries[5]. This approach can be applied several times. The complexity of the protocol can be calculated as follows:

$$P_3 = \frac{N^2 + m^2 + 2(m/2)^2 + 4*(m/4)^2 + ... + 2m^2/m}{m + m/2 + m/4 + m/8 + ... + 1} =$$

$$\frac{N^2 + m^2(1 + 1/2 + 1/4 + ... + 2/m)}{m(1 + 1/2 + 1/4 + 1/8 + ... + 1/m)} \approx$$

$$\frac{N^2 + m^2(1 + 1/2 + 1/4 + ... + 1/m)}{m(1 + 1/2 + 1/4 + 1/8 + ... + 1/m)} =$$

$$\frac{N^2}{m(1 + 1/2 + 1/4 + 1/8 + ... + 1/m)} + m = \frac{N^2}{m(2 - 1/m)} + m \approx \frac{N^2}{2m} + m$$

---

[5] For details, please refer to Section 4.1.

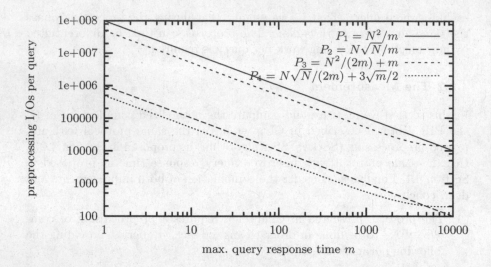

Fig. 4.4. The normalized complexities of the basic protocol [AF01, AF02a], and the two modifications proposed in this chapter are presented as functions of the maximal query response time m, for $N = 10000$.

Finally, we combine the two proposed modifications and measure the normalized complexity of the resulting protocol. Namely, we assume that the shuffling complexity is $O(N\sqrt{N})$ (as proposed in Section 4.2.1), and that the used shuffled databases are refreshed as proposed in Section 4.1. The complexity P_4 of the resulting protocol is then calculated similarly to P_3:

$$P_4 = \frac{N\sqrt{N} + m\sqrt{m} + 2(m/2)\sqrt{m/2} + 4*(m/4)\sqrt{m/4} + ... + 2\sqrt{m}}{m + m/2 + m/4 + m/8 + ... + 1} \approx$$

$$\frac{N\sqrt{N}}{m(1 + 1/2 + 1/4 + 1/8 + ... + 1/m)} + \frac{3\sqrt{m}}{2} \approx \frac{N\sqrt{N}}{2m} + \frac{3\sqrt{m}}{2}$$

To summarize, we show the normalized complexities P_1 through P_4 in Figure 4.4. The approach proposed in Section 4.2.1 reduces the normalized complexity of the PIR protocol from N^2/m to $N\sqrt{N}/m$, whereas the approach proposed in Section 4.1 reduces the normalized complexity of the protocol by a constant factor only.

4.4 Summary

In this chapter we proposed several techniques that improved the query response time or preprocessing complexity of the almost optimal PIR protocol proposed in the previous chapter. We also identified that, among the presented approaches, the improvement of the highest degree comes from substituting the SSA shuffling algorithm with the SSG algorithm proposed in this chapter. However, all calculations of complexities were done in $O()$ notation, discarding (even big) constant factors. The next chapter will experimentally determine the exact performances of SSG, SSA, and a shuffling algorithm from related work.

5 Experimental Analysis of Shuffling Algorithms

The previous chapter proposed a new shuffling algorithm (SSG) and estimated its complexity theoretically. This chapter naturally amplifies the previous chapter with the experimental analysis of the performance of SSG and concurrent approaches (SSA and SBS). Section 5.1 describes a shuffling algorithm from related work (SBS). Section 5.2 explains the experiments we performed to find the best shuffling algorithm among SSA, SSG, and SBS. Section 5.3 focuses on explaining the paradoxical experimental result from Section 5.2.

5.1 Shuffling Based on Bitonic Sort (SBS)

Related work suggests employing sorting networks for shuffling in such a way that the resulting order is not deducible from the data access pattern produced by sorting [GO96]. Indeed, the basic property of sorting networks is that the order of comparisons required to sort an array is data independent. If these comparisons are sequentially performed inside a SC, the sorting order is not revealed, assuming the records are encrypted before leaving the SC after each comparison.

Bitonic sort (also known as Batcher's sort) is the best sorting network with $O(Nlog^2N)$ comparisons [Bat68]. Although there is an $O(NlogN)$ sorting network [AKS83], it possesses a high constant factor, making the bitonic sort preferable for any reasonable N.

5.2 Experiments

It is unclear which one of the two algorithms, SSG or SBS, should be chosen in practice, when shuffling a database. Figure 5.1 suggests, based on the $O()$ notation, that we use SSG for $N < 65000$ and SBS otherwise. However, this suggestion is of a theoretical nature because the $O()$ notation completely ignores the constant factors. For a more accurate analysis we prototyped and evaluated all three shuffling algorithms using an available SC.

D. Asonov: Querying Databases Privately, LNCS 3128, 49–55, 2004.
© Springer-Verlag Berlin Heidelberg 2004

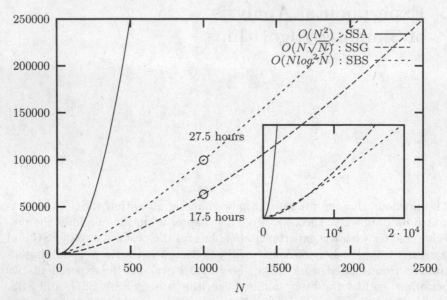

Fig. 5.1. Theoretically estimated complexities for SSA, SSG, and SBS shuffling algorithms.

The exact objective of the experiments was to answer the following questions:

1. Do the complexities of the shuffling algorithms correspond to the theoretically calculated complexities?
2. If the correspondence is not full, what imposes the difference?
3. Of the three available algorithms, which is the most efficient practically?
4. What time is needed to shuffle a sample database using a single secure coprocessor and the best shuffling algorithm?

5.2.1 Setup Details

The experiments were run on a single machine (Intel 686 350 MHz, 256 MB RAM, Linux OS), with a single secure coprocessor installed as a PCI device (IBM 4758-023 with Intel 486 66MHz, 2MB RAM, CP/Q OS).

The general architecture of the prototype is presented in Figure 5.2. We used C programming language to encode both the functions performed by the host and the algorithms running in the coprocessor. The code residing on the host performs I/O requests issued by the coprocessor code and gathers the execution times of the shuffling algorithms. In order to enforce the speed of coding and debugging the algorithms, a coprocessor emulator was programmed and used to develop initial versions of the algorithms.

The tests were run automatically for 24 hours a day for 32 days in the order defined by a test schedule prepared beforehand. The data collected

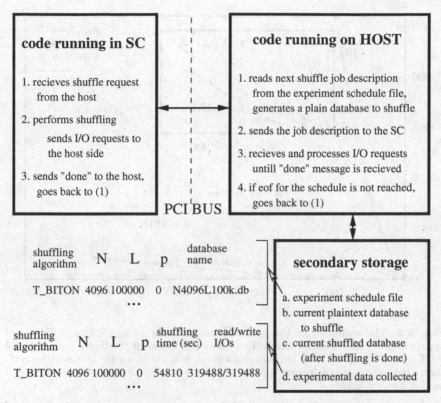

Fig. 5.2. The architecture of the experimental prototype.

is condensed in Figures 5.3 and 5.4 and is discussed and analyzed in the following subsections.

No encryption was used in the algorithms in order to simplify the tests. The encryption module of the IBM 4758 introduces practically no delay in I/O operations: Both with or without encryption the I/O throughout is approximately 1.0 Mbyte/sec.

5.2.2 Experimental Data Collected

Our data was automatically collected from 180 shufflings, performed using different shuffling algorithms and database parameters. Table 5.1 demonstrates the parameter intervals governing the tests conducted.

Figure 5.3 shows how the shuffling time depends on the algorithm type and the number of records in the database N, with the size of a record L and parameter p (for the SSG algorithm) being fixed.

Figure 5.4 is exclusively dedicated to the SSG algorithm, and demonstrates how the shuffling time depends upon the parameter p.

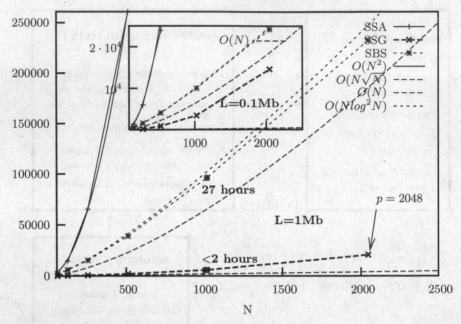

Fig. 5.3. The summary of the performance tests for SSA, SSG, and SBS; and approximating functions for them. The difference between the figure (experiments for $L = 1Mb$) and the inset (experiments for $L = 0.1Mb$) is only observed for SSG algorithm, whose running time approaches $O(N)$ border for $L = 1Mb$ and $O(N^{1.5})$ border for $L = 0.1Mb$.

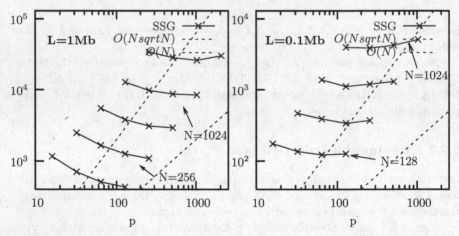

Fig. 5.4. Finding the optimal value for the parameter p of the SSG algorithm experimentally.

Table 5.1. Parameter intervals for the experiments.

algorithm	database parameters		
	N	L	p
SSA	128, 256, 512, 1024, 2048	0.1, 1.0 Mbyte	–
SSG	128, 256, 512, 1024, 2048	0.1, 1.0 Mbyte	$N/8, N/4, N/2, N$
SBS	128, 256, 512, 1024, 2048	0.1, 1.0 Mbyte	–

5.2.3 Analysis

The analysis of the experimental data collected allows us to answer the above questions:

1. The experimental data backs up the expected complexities of the algorithms except for SSG, which performs considerably better than expected. Additionally, the optimal value for SSG's trade-off parameter p differs from the one calculated in theory.
2. We explain the difference between theoretical and practical results for the SSG algorithm separately, in the next subsection (Section 5.3).
3. The SSG algorithm outperformed the rest in all of the tests that took place. However, the preliminary calculations based on experimental data suggest that SBS may dominate SSG for large $N > 5 \cdot 10^6$. This preliminary number was obtained by intersecting the approximation functions for SBS and SSG in the case of $L = 1Mb$.
4. With a single SC, less than 2 hours are needed for shuffling a database of 1000 records of 1 Mb each, using the most efficient algorithm available (SSG). This compares to 294 hours or 26 hours needed for shuffling the same database using SSA or SBS, respectively.

5.3 The Superiority of SSG

We now discuss two issues related to the unexpected high performance of SSG revealed by the experiments.

First, we explain which assumptions in Section 4.2.1 led to the partial disagreement between theoretical and experimental results for SSG. In particular, we show that under some refined assumptions, SSG performs shuffling in linear time.

Second, we discuss why linear shuffling time is possible at all. Namely, we argue that the problem is easier than sorting, and thus is solvable in linear time in some cases.

5.3.1 Imperfection of the Theoretically Estimated Complexity of SSG

In Section 4.2.1 we theoretically estimated the complexity of SSG to be $O(N\sqrt{N})$. However, the experiments show that the real complexity of SSG varies between $O(N\sqrt{N})$ and $O(N)$ (see Figure 5.3), depending on the database parameters. We enumerate the simplifications made during the estimation, which led to the imperfection of the theoretical results:

1. We assumed the disk I/O speed to be the same as the SC I/O speed. In fact, disk I/Os are faster (at factor 10 to 30) than SC I/Os. SSA and SBS perform all I/O operations through the SC, thus this difference plays no role and corresponding experimental data agree with the theory. SSG uses the SC for only a part of its I/O operations (shuffling) and does the rest of the operations (gathering) using the disk only. So these latter I/O operations of SSG perform at considerably higher speed than SSA and SBS I/Os, leading to a better performance from SSG than predicted.

2. We counted $O(pN)$ different I/Os during the splitting and gathering parts of SSG, but we ignored that the size of each of these I/Os is p times smaller than the I/Os used by SSA, SBS, and the shuffling part of SSG. This improves the actual performance of SSG and pushes the optimal value for p higher. Thus, the theoretically calculated optimal value for parameter $p = \sqrt{N}$ for the SSG algorithm is far less than the experimentally observed one ($p \approx N$, Figure 5.4).

3. We assumed that the speed of an I/O operation (in bytes per second) does not depend on the number of bytes transmitted by this I/O. However, this assumption does not hold for I/Os with a small number of bytes. The I/Os speeds for (i) the disk, and (ii) especially for the SC, are slower for I/Os with smaller number of bytes if this number is $< 10Kb$ [1]. Both the former and latter affect the speed of SSG for $L = 0.1Mb$ significantly, because SSG operates with I/Os of L/p size. For $L = 1Mb$ this effect is less significant. This is why the performance of SSG for $L = 0.1Mb$ does not resemble the performance for $L = 1Mb$, as can be seen on Figure 5.3. On the other hand, the dynamics of SSA and SBS for $L = 0.1Mb$ is the same as for $L = 1Mb$, because the I/O size (L) they are dealing with is larger than $10Kb$.

We conclude that the theoretically estimated complexity $O(N\sqrt{N})$ provides only an upper bound for the real complexity of SSG, due to simplifications made in the theoretical calculations. Thus, SSG shuffles in $O(N\sqrt{N})$ time in a worst case only, for very large N and small L. Otherwise the complexity is lower, approaching $O(N)$ for large L or moderate N.

5.3.2 On Minimal Bound for Shuffling Complexity

As discussed in Section 5.1, shuffling a database privately can be performed by using a sorting network. The sorting network of the best performance is

---

[1] The reason for the former is known to the database community: Seeking a disk position takes equal time for different sizes of records; and seeking time is negligible as the chunks become larger. The reason for the latter is the device driver of a SC, which is optimized for large chunks.

the bitonic sort of $O(Nlog^2N)$ complexity. The natural question arises: Why is a shuffling algorithm (SSG) that outperforms a bitonic sort (SBS) possible?

We offer a simple answer: It is possible because using a sorting network is not always the optimal way to approach the shuffling problem. That is, the minimal bound for the sorting network problem is not true for private shuffling. For example, in the previous subsection we observed that the SSG algorithm reaches $O(N)$ complexity for certain databases, whereas SBS remains at $O(Nlog^2N)$ complexity.

5.4 Summary

In this chapter we reported our experimental results for three shuffling algorithms. The SSG algorithm proposed in the previous chapter is the superior one, shuffling a sample database of 1000 records 1 Mb each in just 2 hours, compared to 26 hours shuffling time for the nearest competitor from related work. Experimental data collected significantly helped us to better estimate the complexity of SSG, which is surprisingly approaching linear time for some types of databases.

It seems likely that it is possible to reduce the shuffling times of all the three algorithms by an order of magnitude if some specifics of the IBM 4758 architecture are taken into account to increase the I/O throughput of the SC [Per02, LS01].

Part III

Generalizing the PIR Model

6 Repudiative Information Retrieval

Existing PIR algorithms reveal no information about a query, nor its results. In this chapter we propose an algorithm that gives the user a choice in the trade-off between the protocol complexity and the amount of privacy. After the introduction, Section 6.2 defines the relaxed privacy (repudiation) and a measure to assess the quality of privacy (robustness of repudiation). Section 6.3 demonstrates a basic Repudiative Information Retrieval (RIR) protocol with constant robustness of repudiation. Then we show how to construct a RIR protocol with any given robustness of repudiation in Section 6.4. In particular, we identify conditions that turn our RIR protocol into PIR. Finally, we mention the related work and discuss some questionable points of our approach.

6.1 The Need for Trade-Off between Privacy and Complexity

Important characteristics of a PIR protocol from the user's point of view are (i) communication complexity between the user and server, and (ii) the query response time. Initially proposed PIR protocols possess high complexity in either communication between the server and user [BDF00, SJ00] or query response time [KO97, CMS99, SS00, SS01, KY01]. An effort to achieve optimal both communication and query response time results in heavy periodical preprocessing. $O(N \log N)$ I/Os are required for preprocessing before answering a query (if the SBS preprocessing algorithm is used; Chapter 5 provides details). With some realistic assumptions it takes the server several minutes of preprocessing to prepare for answering one query, rendering it intolerable for dynamic business applications.

A natural question arises as to whether it is possible to reduce the preprocessing complexity by relaxing the strong privacy requirement from "*no information about queries is revealed*" to "*not much information about queries is revealed*".

By "not much", we mean that even if some information is revealed, an observer cannot determine for sure if the user queried the 1-st, the 2-nd, the

D. Asonov: Querying Databases Privately, LNCS 3128, 59–75, 2004.
© Springer-Verlag Berlin Heidelberg 2004

3-rd, ..., or the N-th record. That is, the user can deny any claims of the form "the record you queried is [not] the j-th record", for any j. If a protocol provides users with this repudiation property, we call it a Repudiative Information Retrieval (RIR) protocol.

Apart from theoretical interest, such protocols would be valuable in practical scenarios where, provided that the repudiation property is preserved, users agree to sacrifice some privacy for better performance.

6.1.1 Our Results

In this chapter', we show that if "not much" information should be revealed, $O(\sqrt{N})$ preprocessing complexity is achievable when keeping communication and query response time optimal. In other words, we construct a RIR protocol with optimal communication and query response time, and $O(\sqrt{N})$ preprocessing complexity per query (in contrast to $O(N \log N)$ preprocessing complexity required for PIR).

6.1.2 Preliminaries and Assumptions

The database model and the query type remain identical to those in the PIR model[1]. The only change we introduce is that some information about the content of the query may be revealed. We denote this information $I_{revealed}$. This information is determined by the specific protocol used.

6.2 Defining Repudiation and Assessing Its Robustness

We define whether or not the repudiation property is supported by a given protocol in Section 6.2.1. For the cases where the repudiation property is supported, we suggest the assessment of this property's robustness in Section 6.2.2.

6.2.1 Repudiation Property

Let us assume that the user has run a protocol to execute his query $q =$ "return the i-th record", or $q = i$ for short. We say that this protocol assures the repudiation property if q can be of any value between 1 and N for an observer. Therefore, the user can deny any claim of the type "the record you queried is [not] the j-th record". Formally, the repudiation property is preserved iff:

---

[1] Namely, we consider a model where users query a database of N records. The content of a user query is presumed to be of the form "return the i-th record". By observer, we mean (anyone in conspiracy with) the database server that exclusively accesses the database, trying to figure out the content of the user query.

$$0 < P(q = j|I_{revealed}) < 1, \quad \forall j : 1 \le j \le N \tag{6.1}$$

That is, given the information $I_{revealed}$ revealed by the protocol that provides the repudiation property, it must be impossible to exclude any record from being a target of the user query. If the protocol provides the repudiation property, we call it a repudiative information retrieval (RIR) protocol. Examples of probability distributions $P(q = x)$ provided by different hypothetical protocols[2] are shown in Figure 6.1 for $N = 5$.

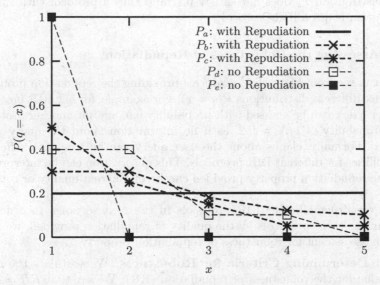

Fig. 6.1. The probability distributions with or without repudiation property.

Now that we defined RIR, it is important to clearly understand the relationship between RIR, PIR, and a simple retrieval of the required record without any privacy techniques. We call the former a download for short. All three are compared in Table 6.1 based on the distributions $P(q|I_{revealed})$ they produce. Distribution P_e belongs to a download protocol because all information about query q is revealed, i.e., Shannon's entropy $H(P_e) = 0$. Distributions P_a, P_b, P_c, P_d represent protocols that hide some information about the query. $P_a, P_b,$ and P_c are produced by RIR protocols (labeled as RIR_N in the table), so the user can decline any claims "the record you queried is [not] the j-th record" for any $1 \le j \le N$. Note that distribution P_a, although representing a RIR protocol, can also be classified for a PIR protocol because no information about the query is revealed in this distribu-

---

[2] The probabilities in the distributions on the figure are sorted (in the descending order) to make it easier to compare the possible patterns of distributions.

Table 6.1. Possible probability distributions classified.

Protocol	Parameter			
	distribution $P(q)$	repudiation assured	preprocess. complexity	info kept private
Download	P_e	no	0	$H(P) = 0$
PIR_N	P_a	yes	$O(N log N)$	$H(P) =$ max
RIR_N	P_a, P_b, P_c	yes	?	$0 < H \leq$ max
$RIR_{n<N}$	P_d	no	?	$0 < H <$ max

tion. Distribution P_d does not satisfy 6.1, and thus a protocol with such a distribution is not a RIR protocol[3].

6.2.2 Assessing the Robustness of Repudiation

As we can see from Figure 6.1, protocols providing the repudiation property may have different distributions $P(q = x)$. For example, for one RIR protocol the user query can be guessed with probability 0.5, and for another protocol with probability of $1/N = 0.2$, as if no information about the query were revealed. Formally, claims about the user query can be true with different probabilities for different RIR protocols. This observation can be interpreted as if the repudiation property provided can be of different quality or robustness[4].

We construct different RIR protocols in the next sections. In order to differentiate these protocols by the quality of repudiation provided, we may need an assessment for robustness of repudiation property.

6.2.2.1 Determining Criteria for Robustness. We postulate the minimal value for the robustness of repudiation (RR): We say that $RR = 0$ iff repudiation (as defined in the previous section) is not preserved. We say that the robustness of repudiation is maximal ($RR = 1$) iff no information about the query is revealed. Thus, a RIR protocol with $RR = 1$ is a PIR protocol. For example, we presume for the probability distributions shown in Figure 6.1 that:

$$RR(P_a) = 1; \quad RR(P_d) = 0; \quad RR(P_e) = 0$$

$$0 < RR(P_b) < 1; \quad 0 < RR(P_c) < 1$$

In our definition of the criteria for robustness, we must decide how to assess $RR(P)$ in the open interval $]0, 1[$. For instance, we must decide on values for $RR(P_b)$ and $RR(P_c)$. This decision determines, for example, which of

---

[3] However, such a distribution could belong to a RIR protocol if the number of records in the database is reduced from 5 to 4. We denote protocols producing such distributions as $RIR_{n<N}$ and do not consider them in this book. Please refer to Section 6.6.1 for more discussion on the subject.

[4] The meaning of the word robustness in statistical analysis is different from one in plain English. Please do not be confused: We use the word robustness as in plain English; it can be substituted with a synonym like quality.

the two protocols (corresponding to distributions P_b and P_c) provides more robust repudiation. Our approach towards assessing $RR(P)$ in the interval $]0, 1[$ is as follows.

We show how to obtain any distribution P by incrementally morphing the perfect distribution P_a that corresponds to $RR = 1$. Specifically, the morphing is performed by applying a number of elementary changes. An elementary change is made by altering only two points in the distribution. This is done by adding some $\delta > 0$ to one probability and subtracting δ from another one.

Intuitively, a good assessment function $RR(P)$ must monotonically decrease as the distribution is being morphed from P_a to P, because the distribution moves further away from the perfect distribution with each new change (Figure 6.2).

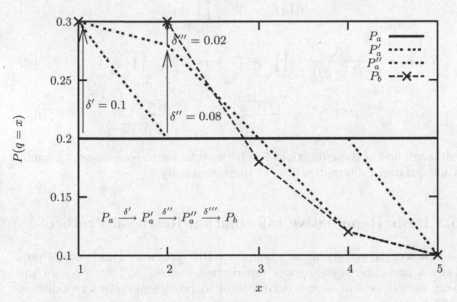

Fig. 6.2. The distribution P_a is morphed into P_b through three elementary changes. Each change increases the difference between the current distribution and P_a.

In summary, we postulate that the following three properties are necessary and sufficient for a function (RR) to serve as an assessment of the repudiation robustness of a protocol:

1. $RR(P) = 0$ iff $\exists i : \quad p_i = 0 \quad (or \quad p_i = 1)$
2. $RR(P) = 1$ iff $\forall i : \quad p_i = \frac{1}{N}$
3. $\forall P = \{p_1, p_2, ..., p_N\}, \quad P' = \{p_1 + \delta, p_2 - \delta, ..., p_N\}, \quad p_1 \geq p_2 :$
   $RR(P) > RR(P')$

In the example of Figure 6.2, the third property implies that for any function $RR(P)$ eligible for assessing robustness of repudiation it must hold:

$$RR(P_a) > RR(P'_a) > RR(P''_a) > RR(P_b)$$

The task now is to find a function satisfying all three criteria.

6.2.2.2 Function Satisfying The Criteria. An example of a function satisfying all the three criteria is:

$$RR(P) \underset{def}{=} N^2 \frac{1}{\sum_{1 \leq i \leq N} \frac{1}{p_i}} \qquad (6.2)$$

Other functions satisfying the three criteria include, for instance:

$$RR(P) = N^N \prod_{1 \leq i \leq N} p_i \qquad (6.3)$$

$$RR(P) = \frac{1}{(\frac{1}{N}(1 - \frac{1}{N}))^N} \prod_{1 \leq i \leq N} p_i(1 - p_i) \approx eN^N \prod_{1 \leq i \leq N} p_i(1 - p_i) \qquad (6.4)$$

$$RR(P) = \frac{N\frac{1}{\frac{1}{N}(1-\frac{1}{N})}}{\sum_{1 \leq i \leq N} \frac{1}{p_i(1-p_i)}} = \frac{\frac{N^3}{N-1}}{\sum_{1 \leq i \leq N} \frac{1}{p_i(1-p_i)}} \qquad (6.5)$$

Although any of these functions can be used to assess robustness of repudiation, we prefer alternative 6.2 due to its simplicity.

6.3 Basic Repudiative Information Retrieval Protocol

In this section we present an example of RIR protocol. This protocol provides a particular robustness of repudiation, namely $RR = O(\frac{1}{N})$. In the next section we will extend our protocol to provide any given repudiation robustness.

Similar to the PIR protocols proposed in Part II of this book and in [SS00, SS01, AF01, AF02a], our RIR protocol uses the notion of a secure coprocessor (SC). We recall that, from a theoretical point of view, the notion of SC can be substituted with the notion of the third party that (i) runs the protocol certified by users and the server, (ii) cannot alter this protocol, and (iii) discloses nothing above what the protocol specifies to disclose. Consequently, the data processed inside the SC cannot be observed from outside of the SC. For a more detailed introduction, we sketched a simple PIR protocol based on SC in Section 2.2.4.

A basic RIR protocol is provided by Algorithm 8 that runs inside a SC (Figure 6.4). Before starting this protocol, the SC must prepare database RS

Input: The database of N records $DB[1, ..., N]$; a database of randomly selected
    (encrypted) records $RS[1, ...]$; a number of previously answered queries k; a
    record's number to retrieve i;
Output: $DB[i]$: i-th record of the database DB;
  1: $read\_into\_SC(Result \Leftarrow decrypt(RS[k+1]))$
  2: **if** $index(RS[k+1]) == i$ **then**
  3:     $Range = \{1, ..., N\} \setminus \{i\}$
  4:     $h = select\_random\_from(Range)$ {Select randomly one of the records
                                                         referred to in $Range$}
  5:     $read\_into\_SC(Temp \Leftarrow DB[h])$
  6: **else**
  7:     $read\_into\_SC(Result \Leftarrow DB[i])$
  8: **end if**
  9: $k = k + 1$
 10: $output\_from\_SC(encrypt(Result))$ {Encrypt and output $Result$ from the SC}

Algorithm 8: An example of a RIR protocol.

which later is used as an input for Algorithm 8. Each record in RS is randomly
selected from the original database. Each record is also kept encrypted with
the SC's private key, so that no one can determine its identity. Algorithm 8
takes one previously not accessed record from RS to answer one query. Thus,
the database RS must be renewed periodically.

In the rest of this section we (i) analyze the robustness of repudiation of
the proposed protocol, (ii) consider the case for multiple queries, and (iii)
discuss the complexity of preparing x records for the database RS.

6.3.1 Analyzing the Robustness of the Protocol

The basic idea behind Algorithm 8 is the following. As the SC receives the
query, the SC decrypts it, and obtains i – the number of a record desired
by the user. Then the SC reads the next unused record from RS, decrypts
it, and checks if it is the record requested by the user. If yes, the SC reads
a randomly selected record from the original database DB, but sends the
read RS record as a query response, encrypted with the user key. If no, the
SC reads the desired record directly from DB, and sends it as a response,
encrypted. The former and latter outcomes have probabilities of $1/N$ and
$(N-1)/N$, correspondingly:

$$P(q = index(RS[k+1])) = \frac{1}{N} = P(q \neq d) \qquad (6.6)$$

$$P(q = d) = \frac{N-1}{N} \qquad (6.7)$$

where function $index(RS[k+1])$ denotes the number of the record from the
original database DB, that record $RS[k+1]$ represents in an encrypted form;
d denotes the record number read by the SC from DB to answer a query.

The probability distribution $P_{sect3}(q = x)$ provided by our protocol is shown in Figure 6.3. This protocol is repudiative, i.e., equation 6.1 holds, because an observer can neither reject nor prove that the record of interest to the user was record number j, for all $1 \le j \le N$.

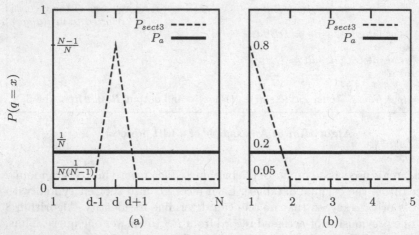

Fig. 6.3. (a) An example of probability distribution corresponding to the proposed RIR protocol. (b) The distribution pattern for $N = 5$ (with ordered probabilities).

Not surprisingly, robustness of repudiation provided by our protocol is less than perfect:

$$RR(P_{sect3}) = \frac{N^2}{\sum\limits_{1 \le i \le N} \frac{1}{p_i}} = \frac{N^2}{N(N-1)^2 + \frac{N}{N-1}} = O\left(\frac{1}{N}\right) < RR(P_a) = 1$$

$$(6.8)$$

6.3.2 Multiple Queries

The amount of information revealed remains zero for PIR (and for RIR protocols with full robustness of repudiation) as the number of answered queries grows. Several questions arise when considering a RIR protocol with $RR < 1$ executing several queries, because in this case the amount of information revealed is not zero, and may grow with the number of queries answered. If a user queries a database several times using a RIR protocol, then:

1. Does the shape of the probability distribution $P(q = x)$ change from query to query?
2. Does the probability of a given record (number s) to be accessed by at least one of the queries increase with the number of queries answered? If yes, does it reach 1 for some number of queries?

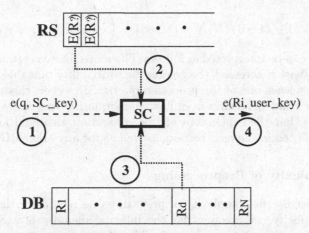

Fig. 6.4. Scheme of a RIR protocol.

The shape of the probability distribution $P(q = x)$ does not change from query to query, because the queries are executed independently of each other. Independently from the number of queries answered, the distribution $P(q = x)$ is of the same form for all queries[5]. The repudiation property holds for every query answered.

To answer the second question, we assume that k queries have been answered. Formally, we are looking for the probability:

$$p_{s,k} \underset{def}{=} P(q_1 = s, \text{ or } q_2 = s, ..., \text{ or } q_k = s) =$$
$$1 - P(q_1 \neq s, \text{ and } q_2 \neq s, ..., \text{ and } q_k \neq s) =$$
$$1 - P(q_1 \neq s) \cdot P(q_2 \neq s) \cdot ... \cdot P(q_k \neq s) \quad (6.9)$$

This probability grows with k, even if no information is revealed. However, $p_{s,k}$ never reaches 1. As a consequence, the robustness of repudiation associated with the distribution $(p_{s,k}, 1 - p_{s,k})$ never reaches 0 even if all of the user queries are equal. For example, in the case of PIR it holds for $p_{s,k}$:

$$p_{s,k}^{\mathrm{PIR}} = 1 - (1 - 1/N)^k = 1 - \left(\frac{N-1}{N}\right)^k, \quad \forall s$$

To provide another example, we consider the RIR protocol described in this section. We also assume that for all k queries the SC reads the record number d' from the open database. Then, based on equation 6.9 we obtain:

$$p_{s,k} = 1 \quad (1 - (N-1)/N)^k = 1 - \frac{1}{N^k}, \quad for \ s = d'$$

---

[5] For the protocol presented above, this form is depicted in Figure 6.3.

$$p_{s,k} = 1 - (1 - 1/(N(N-1))) \approx 1 - \left(\frac{N^2 - 1}{N^2}\right)^k, \ \forall \ s \neq d'$$

This formula can be interpreted as follows. The more times a certain record in the open database is accessed, the greater the probability that this record was a target for at least one of the processed queries. However, this probability never reaches 1 independently from how many queries were answered.

We notice that the conclusions of this subsection also hold for the RIR protocol presented in the next section, as well as for any other RIR protocol.

6.3.3 Complexity of Preprocessing

We briefly discuss the complexity of preparing one record for the database RS. For simplicity, we assume that the internal memory of a SC is large enough to store $O(1)$ database records. The straightforward approach is to read the entire database through the SC, but select one random record to keep inside the SC. After the entire database is read through, the SC outputs the encrypted record and stores it in the database RS. Since the SC must read N database records, the upper bound for the I/O complexity of preparing one record for RS is $O(N)$. However, a better complexity can be achieved if the SSG algorithm is used to generate an RS database[6]. SSG builds a database of N records using $O(N\sqrt{N})$ I/Os[7]. This database would be used to answer N queries, resulting in a preprocessing complexity of $O(\sqrt{N})$ I/Os per query.

6.3.4 Summary of the Basic RIR

We have constructed a RIR protocol with both query response time and communication of $O(1)$ complexity. The preprocessing complexity is $O(\sqrt{N})$ per query, compared to $O(NlogN)$ for PIR with the same query response time and communication. However, the user might be dissatisfied with the low robustness provided by the protocol above. We therefore extend our RIR protocol to provide any specific robustness of repudiation.

6.4 Varying the Robustness of the RIR Protocol

This section considers the problem of constructing RIR protocols with a given robustness between 0 and 1. Specifically, the first part of this section presents a RIR protocol with two parameters. Next, we show that by varying these

---

[6] More precisely, a straightforward modification must be applied to the SSG algorithm for it to handle the specific characteristics of the RS database.

[7] As it was explained in Chapter 5, $O(N\sqrt{N})$ I/O complexity is the upper bound for the complexity of SSG, because SSG provides higher performance for certain types of databases. However, in this chapter we will ignore this fact and will only consider the worst case complexity of SSG.

parameters, a robustness between 0 and 1 can be achieved. In particular, we show which parameters cause this protocol to gain full robustness, thus turning it into a PIR protocol.

6.4.1 A Parameterized RIR Protocol

We present Algorithm 9 as an extension of Algorithm 8 (see also Figure 6.5). The only difference between the two is that in the extended version, the SC reads α records from the RS database and β records ($DB[d_1], ..., DB[d_\beta]$) from the DB database, whereas $\alpha = \beta = 1$ for the basic protocol presented earlier. The query response time of the protocol is $O(\alpha + \beta)$, and the preprocessing complexity per query is $O(\alpha\sqrt{N})$.

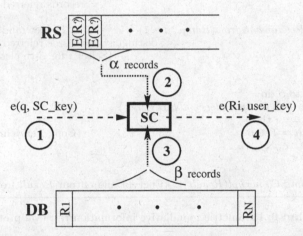

Fig. 6.5. A RIR protocol with configurable robustness of repudiation.

6.4.2 How Parameters Determine Robustness of Repudiation

Our goal is to see how robustness of repudiation depends on α and β parameters of the protocol. In order to find the protocol's robustness of repudiation, we first calculate the probability distribution $P(q = x)$.

The probability of the query not being among $d_1, ..., d_\beta$ is equal to the probability of finding the required record among the α records read from RS:

$$P(q \notin \{d_1, ..., d_\beta\}) = P(q \in \{index(RS[k+1, ..., k+\alpha])\}) = 1 - \left(\frac{N-1}{N}\right)^\alpha$$

$$(6.10)$$

The probability of the query being among $d_1, ..., d_\beta$ is calculated as:

$$P(q \in \{d_1, ..., d_\beta\}) = 1 - P(q \notin \{d_1, ..., d_\beta\}) = \left(\frac{N-1}{N}\right)^\alpha \qquad (6.11)$$

Input: The database of N records $DB[1, ..., N]$; a database of randomly selected
(encrypted) records $RS[1, ...]$; a number of previously answered queries k; a
record's number to retrieve i; α and β - parameters of the protocol;
Output: $DB[i]$: i-th record of the database DB;
```
 1: GotResult = no
 2: for g = 1 to α do
 3:    read_into_SC(Temp ⇐ decrypt(RS[k * α + g]))
 4:    if index(RS[k + 1]) == i then
 5:       Result = Temp                          {Copy Temp into Result}
 6:       GotResult = yes
 7:    end if
 8: end for
 9: Range = {1, ..., N} \ {i}
10: if GotResult == yes then
11:    H = select_random_from(Range, β)    {Select randomly β distinguished
                                              records referred in Range}
12: else
13:    H = select_random_from(Range, β − 1)        {Select randomly β − 1
                                       distinguished records referred in Range}
14:    H[β] = i                     {Select i for β-th element in H}
15: end if
16: sort(H)
17: for g = 1 to β do
18:    read_into_SC(Temp ⇐ decrypt(DB[H[g]]))
19:    if H[g] == i then
20:       Result = Temp                          {Copy Temp into Result}
21:    end if
22: end for
23: k = k + 1
24: output_from_SC(encrypt(Result))  {Encrypt and output Result from the SC}
```

Algorithm 9: Parametric repudiative information retrieval protocol.

Now, we obtained values for $P(q = x)$ for all $1 \leq x \leq N$ (Figure 6.6a):

$$P(q = x) = \frac{1}{\beta}\left(\frac{N-1}{N}\right)^{\alpha}, \quad \forall x \in \{d_1, ..., d_\beta\} \tag{6.12}$$

$$P(q = x) = \frac{1}{N-\beta}\left(1 - \left(\frac{N-1}{N}\right)^{\alpha}\right), \forall x \notin \{d_1, ..., d_\beta\} \tag{6.13}$$

Finally, we can calculate robustness of repudiation as a function of α and β,
also shown in Figure 6.7:

$$RR(\alpha, \beta) = \frac{N^2}{\sum_{1 \leq i \leq N} \frac{1}{p_i}} = \frac{N^2}{\frac{(N-\beta)^2}{1-\left(\frac{N-1}{N}\right)^{\alpha}} + \frac{\beta^2}{\left(\frac{N-1}{N}\right)^{\alpha}}} \tag{6.14}$$

Note that for $\alpha = \beta = 1$, equation 6.14 is identical to equation 6.8.

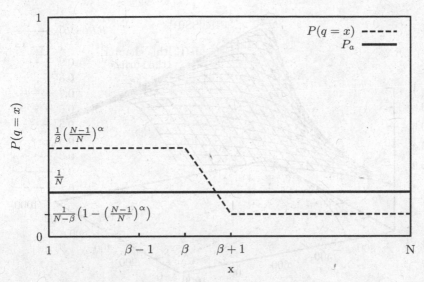

Fig. 6.6. The distribution $P(q = x)$ for given α, β; probabilities are ordered. (Note that this graph looks different for different α, β.)

6.4.3 Turning the RIR Protocol into a PIR Protocol

This subsection determines α and β such that our RIR protocol can be viewed as a PIR protocol. We look for α and β such that our RIR protocol reveals no information about the query. No information is revealed when and only when distributions $P(q = x)$ and P_a are identical in Figure 6.6:

$$\frac{1}{N} = \frac{1}{\beta}\left(\frac{N-1}{N}\right)^\alpha = \frac{1}{N-\beta}\left(1 - \left(\frac{N-1}{N}\right)^\alpha\right)$$

$$[t]\beta = (N-1)\left(\frac{N-1}{N}\right)^{\alpha-1} \tag{6.15}$$

Figure 6.8 exhibits the equation above, and shows the relationship between α and β by which our protocol performs like a PIR protocol.

It can be shown that the response time $O(\alpha + \beta)$ of the protocol is equal to or higher than $O(N)$. This fact makes the use of this RIR protocol for PIR inefficient, because response times of the original PIR protocols range from $O(1)$ to $O(N)$ [AF02a, CMS99, SS01].

6.5 Related Work

So far, the literature has not reported any work on relaxing privacy requirements for PIR. However, some research that can still be related to our work does exist.

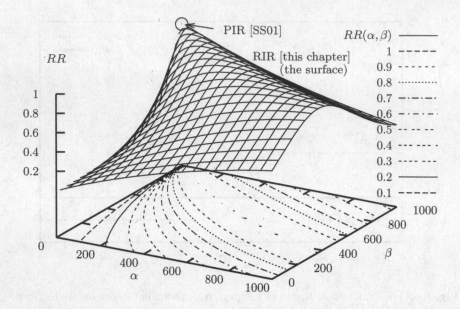

Fig. 6.7. Robustness of repudiation of a RIR protocol is a function of α and β ($N = 1000$).

6.5.1 Deniable Encryption

Encryption is deniable [CDNO97, Riv98] if several (or even any) cleartexts can be thought of as a source of a given encrypted message. Repudiative information retrieval is similar to deniable encryption, in that any of the database records can be thought of as a user query target.

6.5.2 Alternatives to the Quantification of Repudiation

Different formalizations of anonymity have been proposed recently [SH02, Shm02, SS99, SD02, DSCP02]. Most of these are designed to compare the quality of different anonymizing networks or services.

We cannot apply these approaches to formalize the robustness of repudiation provided by a RIR protocol because the subjects differ principally. Anonymity approaches aim to hide identities of the acting users, while RIR (with PIR as its extreme form) aims to hide the actions performed by identifiable users. To support the latter, we provided an original quantification for the repudiation property of RIR, as described above.

An alternative approach to designing quantification for repudiation is to consider existing measures of distance between probability distributions [GS02]. Given the probability distribution $P(q = x) = P_a$ of PIR as a standard, one could measure the distances between P_a and any P_{x1} and P_{x2} in order to compare the robustness of repudiation associated with P_{x1} and P_{x2}.

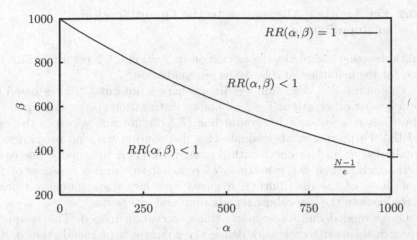

Fig. 6.8. Determining α and β that correspond to a PIR protocol ($N = 1000$).

We have examined several known measures of distance, and concluded that these measures are inconvenient to use as a repudiation measure for several reasons. The main reason is that an RR function based on those measures would not satisfy the three properties defined in Section 6.2.2.

Finally, we note that Shannon's entropy measure is unsuitable for measuring the robustness of repudiation. This is because the entropy of a distribution P with $p_i = 0$ (for some i) is not necessarily 0, whereas the robustness of repudiation must be zero in this case as is defined by equation 6.1.

6.6 Discussion

This section is mainly motivated by the questions raised by the WPES'02 auditorium on November 21, 2002.

6.6.1 Redefining Repudiation

We say that the repudiation property is preserved if the observer cannot eliminate *any* of the N items as a possible result of the query. A related question is this: What happens if we substitute the word "any" in the previous sentence with "some $z < N$"? In other words, one might consider a more relaxed definition of repudiation, with a certain number (z) of points in the probability distribution being allowed to be equal to 0.

We did not investigate this relaxed definition because all of the conclusions made using our strong definition would repeat themselves for the relaxed case. That is, RIR based on the relaxed definition can be reduced to RIR based on the strong definition of repudiation by simply considering a database of z records for which repudiation (in the strong definition) is provided.

6.6.2 Yet Another Alternative to the Quantification of Repudiation

This subsection completes the discussion in Section 6.5.2 regarding alternatives for the definition of robustness of repudiation.

The alternative definition we discuss here is informal, and is based on the following observation. The probability distribution corresponding to full robustness is a straight horizontal line (P_a, Figure 6.1, which is the case of PIR). Furthermore, an example of a distribution with no robustness of repudiation at all is a curve with a great peak (P_e). Informally, one could alternatively define the robustness of repudiation using a measure of the smoothness of the distribution. A curve with larger and numerous peaks corresponds to the less robust repudiation, and vice versa.

Our formal definition supports this observation indeed. The morphing approach we used to formally define the robustness of repudiation is just another interpretation of the described observation.

6.6.3 Misinforming the Observers

The concept of PIR (RIR) is to reveal no (or partial) information about the user query. Now, one can consider a kind of generalized concept: Let the user and the SC act so that not only all (or part of) *true* information about query content is hidden, but some *false* information about the query content is also revealed to confuse the observer [AD02].

For a better understanding, imagine a user intends to query a digital book with some compromising title XXX. If he queries this item using PIR, no information about the title is revealed. The questions are: (i) Does it make sense (and, (ii) is it possible) to reveal false information about the content of the query to misinform the observer? Misinformation in this context means that it appears as if an item with a neutral title YYY is retrieved with high probability. We believe that these questions require separate and more detailed investigation; however, we will outline some preliminary answers.

Regarding the first question, it is important to recall that we assume the sources of the protocols loaded into the SC to be publicly known. This means, observers (such as the server) will be notified if the protocols are modified to misinform observers. Thus they will not "buy" (or believe) the misinformation, and will view any information revealed with scepticism. From this perspective, such misinformation does not make sense.

Independently from the preliminary answer to the first question, we consider the second one. The RIR protocol proposed in this paper can be easily modified to support the misinforming feature. Namely, instead of randomly choosing β (or $\beta - 1$) records to read from the plaintext $DB[N]$ database, the SC must only choose the records from the items with neutral content (as defined by the user).

6.7 Summary

We relaxed the privacy requirement of the PIR model so that some information about the query may be revealed. However, the information revealed should not be enough to say definitely whether the user retrieved the record number 1, or 2, ... or N. In this way the user is provided with the repudiation property.

We constructed such protocols and we call them Repudiative Information Retrieval protocols (RIR). Our RIR construction can be customized according to the robustness of repudiation required. For a small value of robustness, the preprocessing complexity up to $O(\sqrt{N})$ per query can be achieved, compared to $O(NlogN)$ for PIR with the same query response time and communication.

Full robustness of repudiation of a RIR protocol means PIR, and so our RIR protocol can be chosen to serve as a PIR protocol. However, existing PIR protocols have smaller complexities.

PIR protocols exist as two types: those based on general purpose hardware, and those based on a tamper-proof device. We demonstrated a RIR protocol constructed with the use of a tamper proof device. A practical RIR protocol that does not require a tamper proof device remains to be constructed[8].

---

[8] In fact, constructing a practical PIR protocol without use of a tamper proof device also remains an open issue [AF02a].

7 Digital Rights Management for PIR

This chapter considers the problem of providing digital rights management (DRM) for goods sold by means of PIR. Section 7.1 shows that DRM and PIR cannot coexist perfectly. Furthermore, Section 7.2 demonstrates how applying a straightforward DRM scheme violates user privacy. We construct a protocol that provides for both DRM and user privacy in Section 7.3. In Section 7.4, we expose a trade-off between the quality of DRM and the amount of privacy provided, borrowing the relaxed privacy definition from the previous chapter. Section 7.6 proves that a certain negative property of the proposed privacy–preserving DRM scheme is unavoidable. This result is of independent interest, bringing new insight into the research area of electronic voting.

7.1 The Collision between DRM and PIR

Private Information Retrieval provides an execution of user queries over a database of digital goods such that no information about user queries is revealed, even to the server that actually accesses the digital goods. Thus, the provider of digital goods, although owning the server, can get no information about the content of user queries. All the provider can do is count the number of queries issued by a single user, and charge him on a pay-per-query basis. Of course, a PIR protocol must be designed such that no more than one item per query can be retrieved. It is also assumed that all digital goods cost the same price. As we will show, even if one accepts these assumptions, a serious economical problem remains to be solved in order to actually apply PIR.

In practice, the provider may be required to do more than bill the users on a pay-per-query basis. Namely, he may be required to distribute interests among copyright holders of the sold goods. If PIR is used to sell digital goods the provider has no idea of how to distribute the interests, since he has no information about how many times each digital item is retrieved. Any distribution of interests based on query information reveals some information about query content. If we stick to the PIR model (where information about queries is revealed to no one except for the user), interest distribution is impossible.

D. Asonov: Querying Databases Privately, LNCS 3128, 77–97, 2004.
© Springer-Verlag Berlin Heidelberg 2004

Our goal is to eliminate this conflict between DRM and user privacy, by relaxing the privacy constraint of PIR (i.e., by revealing some information about user queries in order to be able to perform the distribution of interests).

We now recall our definition of relaxed privacy[1]. While revealing the information about queries, we aimed at making the disclosure as harmless as possible to user privacy. Even if some information about queries should be revealed, the users must be able to deny any claims about their queries. Formally speaking, for a database of N digital goods, the users can deny any claims of the type "the record you queried is [not] the j-th record", for any $1 \leq j \leq N$. We introduced this property in the previous chapter, and called it the repudiation property of the protocol. Furthermore, the protocols that provide this property are Repudiative Information Retrieval (RIR) protocols.

In the following sections, we discuss how to distribute royalties in such a way that the repudiation property is provided. Specifically, we start by demonstrating that an obvious way for distributing royalties violates the repudiation property. Next, in Section 7.3 we propose a RIR protocol with royalty distribution. This means, we succeed in distributing the royalties while preserving the repudiation property.

In order to preserve the repudiation property, the distribution of royalties must be inexact. Section 7.4 analyzes the trade-off between the robustness of the repudiation provided and the precision of royalty distribution.

Finally, we identify a considerable drawback of the proposed repudiation–preserving DRM scheme in Section 7.5. Section 7.6 proves this drawback to be unavoidable. Apart from the DRM context, this proof contributes to the research in the area of electronic voting. It is partially for this reason that the proof is conducted using electronic voting terminology.

7.2 DRM without Repudiation

In this section we describe an obvious scheme for distributing royalties. We also show that this scheme does not support user privacy, i.e., the repudiation property is not preserved.

The scheme is based on a generalized PIR model. As in the common PIR model, in a database there are N digital records, each of which can be retrieved by the users using a PIR protocol. The server bills every user on a pay-per-query basis. However, each record is from a different owner, and the server must pay royalties to these owners based on how many times their records were retrieved.

Let us consider how the royalty for an owner of record R_j is calculated. We assume that a PIR protocol uses a SC. The SC has access to the content of all queries processed so far. Therefore, the SC identifies the number of times each of u existing users queried the record R_j (Figure 7.1). It then

---

[1] For the original discussion please refer to Sections 6.1 and 6.2.

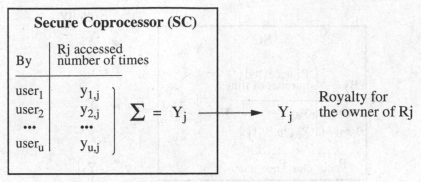

Fig. 7.1. Straightforward royalty distribution with a SC.

adds these numbers to obtain the number of times (Y_j) the record R_j was retrieved:

$$Y_j = y_{1,j} + y_{2,j} + ... + y_{u,j}$$

By calculating such a number for every provider, the SC obtains the vector $< Y_1, ..., Y_N >$, that indicates how many times each record was retrieved, and in which proportion the royalties should be paid to each of the N owners.

Herein, we will refer to Y_j, $\forall 1 \le j \le N$ as a royalty (amount of money) paid to the owner of record R_j. A royalty should not necessarily be calculated as a sum of accesses to the record.

As a result of this simple royalty distribution scheme, the privacy of the user can be violated, even if calculating distribution is hidden by means of the SC. As long as we make no assumptions about the user trusting other users or owners of the records, it is possible for all participants (users and record owners) to cooperate against one user (for example, $user_1$). Then, the number of times this user retrieved a certain record $y_{1,j}$ can be calculated as:

$$y_{1,j} = Y_j - y_{2,j} - ... - y_{u,j}$$

This operation can be performed for each record $1 \le j \le N$, thus providing a complete picture of how many times the $user_1$ queried every record in the database.

One may argue that it is unlikely that all of the users would cooperate against one to violate his privacy. The calculation of $y_{1,j}$ outlined above would then be impossible. However, we argue that all users may indeed cooperate against one user, because they all may turn out to be unreal, generated by the server itself to confuse the SC. There is no reliable technique available that would guarantee a SC or a user that the other users in the protocol really exist. The same is true for the owners of the records.

In conclusion, a straightforward royalty distribution, even if calculated inside a SC, would violate user privacy. To preserve privacy of users, the royalty distribution must be based on a probabilistic function. We propose a probabilistic royalty distribution scheme in the following section.

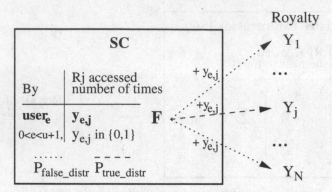

Fig. 7.2. Repudiation–preserving royalty distribution with a SC.

7.3 RIR Supporting DRM

We propose to make the distribution of royalties non-deterministic. Then the observer cannot make any claims about queries with confidence; therefore, the repudiation property would be preserved.

For any executed query $Q = j$, $\forall 1 \le j \le N$, we propose that the SC attaches the royalty to any of the N owners, based on the probability distribution F. Specifically, with the overwhelming probability P_{true_distr} the royalty is assigned to the owner of the record R_j, and with the probability $P_{false\_distr} = (1 - P_{true\_distr})/(N - 1)$ to any of the rest of the owners (Figure 7.2).

For any query, the observer cannot eliminate any of the N records as the query target, even if possessing the information about the distributed royalties.

In the next section we investigate the relationship between the precision of the royalty distribution and the robustness of the repudiation provided.

7.4 Robustness of Repudiation vs. Precision of Royalty Distribution

We employ the measure of the robustness of the repudiation (RR) proposed in the previous chapter (Section 6.2). P_{true_distr} is used as the precision factor for the royalty distribution.

In order to obtain the $RR()$ function, we first discuss the probability distribution $P(Q = x)$ drawn by the observer. We consider only the basic case, when there is only one user posting one query. We assume that after the SC receives the query, it assigns the royalty to the owner of the record R_d. This provides for a straightforward calculation of $P(Q = x)$:

$$p(Q = d) = P_{true\_distr}, \; p(Q = d') = P_{false\_distr} = \frac{(1 - P_{true\_distr})}{N - 1}, \; \forall d' \ne d$$

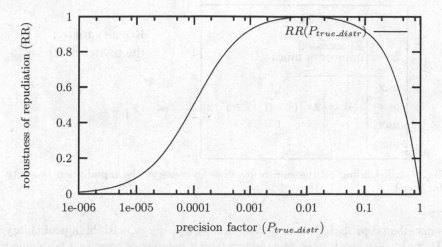

Fig. 7.3. The relationship between precision factor for the royalty distribution and the robustness of repudiation ($N = 100$).

Based on $P(Q = x)$ and the robustness of repudiation definition (equation 6.2 on page 64), we are now able to draw the RR function:

$$RR(P(Q = x)) = \frac{N^2}{\frac{(N-1)^2}{1-P_{true\_distr}} + \frac{1}{P_{true\_distr}}} \tag{7.1}$$

This equation reveals the relationship between robustness of repudiation (RR) and the precision factor of the royalty distribution (P_{true_distr}), depicted in Figure 7.3. This figure agrees with our intuition, in that for more robust repudiation property, sacrificing more precision in the royalty distribution is required. Furthermore, the repudiation property reaches 1 when the precision factor $P_{true\_distr} = 1/N$, i.e., when the royalty is distributed independently from query content.

Another observation is that RR decreases not only for P_{true_distr} approaching 1 but also for P_{true_distr} approaching 0. The reason is that for $P_{true\_distr} = 0$, the observer can claim that the record R_d was not the target of the user query.

In summary, we have formally explained the dependence between the robustness of repudiation and the precision of the royalty distribution. Generally speaking, a DRM of better quality decreases the level of user privacy and vice versa.

7.5 The Drawback of the Proposed DRM Scheme

To identify the drawback associated with the proposed DRM scheme, we consider Figure 7.2 that represents the scheme. The royalty for every query

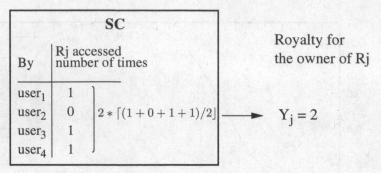

Fig. 7.4. Rounding off the sum of royalties to preserve the repudiation property (for $u = 4$).

is distributed probabilistically. That is, for every query, with high probability (P_{true_distr}) the royalty is assigned to whom it belongs, otherwise it is assigned to anyone from the rest of the owners. Therefore, theoretically speaking, it is not forbidden that an owner receives *no* royalties, even if his record was retrieved a number of times. Instead of him, these royalties may be distributed to the other owners. The drawback of the royalty distribution scheme is that an owner has no guarantee of receiving some minimal portion of the royalties belonging to him.

One might try to avoid this drawback. Let us consider Figure 7.1 on page 79 that presents a royalty distribution scheme without the repudiation property. Furthermore, we describe two attempts of modifying the distribution function (sum) in order for this scheme to preserve repudiation while avoiding the mentioned drawback[2].

The first modification (Figure 7.4) is based on the idea of rounding off the sum of the royalties for a given owner before making it public. Then it is difficult to restore the input of a single user, even if the other inputs and the rounded off sum are known. Specifically, if the inputs $(0, 1, 1)$ of all but the first user and the rounded off sum of the royalties (2) are known, it is still impossible to say whether the input of the $user_1$ was 1 or 0. The reason is that the rounded sum remains the same independently of the input of the $user_1$. Obviously, this royalty distribution approach guarantees that a certain portion of the royalties will be issued to the owner. However, it can be shown that this approach does not preserve the repudiation property[3]. At this point, we only demonstrate an example where the repudiation is broken. Assume that instead of $(0, 1, 1)$, the inputs of the all but the first user are $(1, 1, 1)$. Then, the result is $2 * (\lceil(1 + 1 + 1 + 1)/2\rceil) = 4$. This result is only possible iff the input of $user_1$ is 1. That is, the input of the $user_1$ can be revealed.

---

[2] We call these modifications "attempts", because both will turn out to be unsuccessful.

[3] A formal proof is provided in the following section (Section 7.6.2).

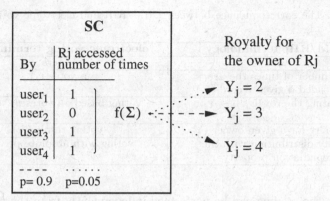

Fig. 7.5. Introducing uncertainty into the royalties to preserve the repudiation property (for $u = 4$).

The second modification (Figure7.5) extends the idea used in the first modification. Namely, instead of rounding off the sum, we propose to vary the result probabilistically. For example, if the sum is 3, we would output the resulting royalty $Y_j = 3$ with high probability, and $Y_j = 2$ and $Y_j = 4$ with lower probability.

With the second modification we avoid the drawback as well: At least $Y_j = 2$ is assigned to the owner if three records of his are retrieved. However, the repudiation property is not preserved for this modification. For $Y_j = 4$, the input of the $user_1$ can be revealed, because $Y_j = 4$ is only possible if the input of the $user_1$ is 1.

The discussion in this section is informal and the arguments are made using examples and counterexamples only. Specifically, we have not proven the general result: A royalty distribution scheme does not exist that preserves the repudiation property and is free of the mentioned drawback. In the next section we formally prove that the drawback explained above is unavoidable if the repudiation is preserved. Surprisingly enough, we found that by proving this statement we also resolve a certain problem in the area of electronic voting. For this reason, we switch to electronic voting terminology while conducting our proof in the next section. Another reason for switching to the electronic voting terminology is to make the discussion easier to follow.

The conventions used for switching from DRM/RIR terminology to electronic voting terminology are shown in Table 7.1. Following these conventions, the statement that we intend to prove can informally be expressed as follows. We assume that all voters can cooperate against one voter to reveal his vote. We also assume that the result is calculated inside a SC, using a given voting function f. Then, for a voting function f that preserves privacy of the voters it must hold: For any fixed set of votes, any voting result is possible. Since this finding is of independent interest, we did our best to present it in such

Table 7.1. The correspondence between DRM/RIR and electronic voting terminology.

DRM/RIR terminology	electronic voting terminology
users	voters
the number of times the $user_i$ downloaded a given record (y_i)	a vote (v_i)
calculating the royalty based on $y_1, ..., y_u$	voting based on votes $v_1, ..., v_N$
the royalty for a given owner (Y)	voting result (R)
royalty distribution with the repudiation property	voting with absolute privacy

a way that the reading can be performed independently from the rest of the book.

7.6 Absolute Privacy in Voting

The problem of privacy in voting (e.g. [CGS97]) is assumed to be a special case of secure multiparty computations [GMW87, Gol99]. That is, the privacy of a voter is presumed to be preserved if the computation of votes is performed in a way that nothing but a result is revealed. This goal is trivially achievable by assuming a third trusted party and private channels between voters and the trusted party. Most of the work on improving privacy in voting is concentrated on achieving the same goal with more and more relaxed cryptographic assumptions [Cha81, CF85, Coh86, Cha88, CFSY96, CGS97].

We claim that achieving the above goal is not sufficient to guarantee a voter that his vote cannot be revealed, even if underlying cryptographic assumptions hold. Namely, there is a second, independent problem: Voters, by cooperating against another voter, may reveal his vote by deducing it from their own votes and the result of voting[4].

Only if both problems are solved, can a voter be sure of his privacy *absolutely*. That is, a voter then can be sure that even if everybody colludes against him, his vote stays private.

Clearly, if simply a sum function is used to calculate the result of voting, then the all-but-one cooperation resolves (and can prove) the vote of a victim by subtracting the sum of their votes from the result. We are interested in finding and investigating functions that "smooth" the result in such a way that the cooperation of all of the other voters cannot prove how the victim voted (or how the victim did not vote – more on this later). Later in

---

[4] This problem was passed over in all the previous work by assuming that the majority would never cooperate to break someone's privacy. The problem is also present in the voting schemes with so-called unconditionally-secret ballots [Cha88] or with information-theoretic privacy [CFSY96].

this chapter, we call such functions "absolutely private voting functions" or "private voting functions" for short.

If we find such functions, we say that the voters are provided with *absolute privacy*, assuming, of course, that the first problem (of calculating a result in such a way that nothing but a result is revealed) is solved too.

Any constant or, alternatively, some function unknown to the participants would be a private voting function. So we require that any voting function we consider cannot be a constant and must be officially known.

One motivation for this problem setting is to find out whether *absolute* privacy exists at all or not. Although such a privacy is recognized to be important[5], we are not aware of any results that deal with absolute privacy in voting.

Along with its academic interest, the "absolutely private voting" setting might be practically applicable in cases where the number of voters is small enough to consider the possibility that all might cooperate against one to break his privacy.

7.6.1 Preliminaries

Normally, the result of a voting is determined by a well-known function that maps a set of casts to a voting result. We prove our theorems only for a particular kind of functions that we call voting functions. A voting function is defined in Sect. 7.6.1.2. A voting function can be deterministic (one set of casts refers to only one result) or probabilistic (one set of casts refers to several results with some probabilities).

Informally, we say that a voter has absolute privacy in voting if no co-operation can break his privacy. His privacy is broken if some cooperation of participants may prove how the voter voted. Privacy is also assumed to be broken if some cooperation may prove how (with what vote) the voter did not vote[6]. This is a privacy violation too because the voter cannot argue anymore that he voted with some arbitrary vote. We give a formal definition and motivation for this kind of privacy later in this section.

We assume that for any cooperation against any voter no information about his cast is known except the voting result. This assumption is shown to be impossible if no special hardware is used [Gol99]. However, this assumption can be made due to the commercially available secure coprocessors that passed FIPS 140-1 Level 4 test (the highest possible rank for a physical and logical protection) [SPW98]. To avoid referring to earlier chapters, we briefly recall that such a device provides the calculation of any function in such a way that nothing but a result is revealed to several independent parties that

---

[5] It is said in [Ger00]: "Voter privacy must be fail-safe - i.e., it must be assured even if everything fails, everyone colludes and there is a court order to reveal all election data."

[6] These two cases are the same, if two casts are possible only (like yes/no).

provide inputs for this function. From the theoretical point of view, we assume a third trusted party (a secure coprocessor), that processes privately the result of a voting out of given votes.

We also assume that the result of a voting is made public after the voting. Figure 7.6 demonstrates the basic architecture of the voting system that we consider.

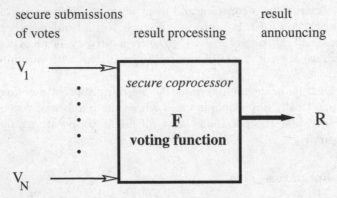

secure submissions
of votes   result processing

result
announcing

Fig. 7.6. Private voting using a secure coprocessor.

7.6.1.1 Our Results. We prove that:

1. Absolute privacy is not possible for deterministic voting functions (Sect. 7.6.2, Theorem 7.6.2). That is, if one wants to have only one result possible for the given casts, one never gains absolute privacy in voting.
2. Absolute privacy is possible for probabilistic voting functions (Sect. 7.6.3, Theorem 7.6.3). We give an example. Simply speaking, we show how to conduct voting such that every voter has absolute privacy.
3. All (probabilistic) voting functions that preserve absolute privacy have a well-recognized drawback (Sect. 7.6.3, Theorem 7.6.4). Namely, all results must be assigned to every set of casts with non-zero probabilities, i.e., for any set of casts any result is possible.

7.6.1.2 Voting Function. The voting function is formally defined as a function that satisfies the properties listed below. These three properties (we call them influence, commutativity, and openness) are used later to prove our results.

By N we denote the number of voters. R denotes the voting result. The (values of) casts of participants are denoted by $v_1, ..., v_N$. The arguments of the function represent the casts of voters and are the values from the set V, the number of elements in the set is $|V|$. The number of possible results is denoted by $|R|$. For short, below we write $\forall v_x$ instead of $\forall v_x \in V$.

Property 1: Influence. Voters must have an *influence* on the result of voting, i.e.

$$\forall v_1, ..., v_N \quad \exists j \leqslant N, v_1', ..., v_j' \quad :$$
$$F(v_1, ..., v_N) \neq F(v_1', ..., v_j', v_{j+1}, ..., v_N) \quad (7.2)$$

This means, that a constant is not a good function for voting. However, it does not state that one vote changes the result. Instead, it only states that some group of votes can change the result.

Property 2: Commutativity. By this property we require F to be commutative, i.e.

$$\forall v_1, ..., v_N, 1 \leqslant i < j \leqslant N \quad :$$
$$F(v_1, ..., v_i, ..., v_j, ..., v_N) = F(v_1, ..., v_j, ..., v_i, ..., v_N) \quad (7.3)$$

Property 3: Function Openness. By this property we state that a function definition is known[7]. This property allows us to presume in proofs that an all-but-one cooperation (that, of course, may include organizers) knows how to calculate the result of the function for any given input.

$$\text{One knows } F(v_1, ...v_N) \text{ for any } v_1, ..., v_N . \quad (7.4)$$

Evidently, if nobody knows how the result of a voting is processed, the voting result does not carry any information. We do not consider this case.

Definition 7.6.1 (Voting Function). *A function is a voting function, iff it satisfies properties 7.2, 7.3, and 7.4.*

7.6.1.3 Private Voting Function. In our definition of absolute privacy, any conspiracy against one voter cannot prove that the voter did not vote with a particular value.

We provide the following example to demonstrate our definition. A user has participated in a voting and he is interested in keeping his cast *absolutely* private. If one can prove that he did not vote C given that only three casts were allowed (A, B, C), it would be natural for him to consider this as his privacy violation. There is a more specific example of why our definition of absolute privacy is appropriate: Our definition allows a voter to claim that he voted with any arbitrary cast, while having no fear that someone can prove opposite.

Herein "absolute privacy" and "absolutely private" are often reduced to "privacy" and "private". In this chapter, we do not consider any privacy, except absolute one.

---

[7] This is a voting scheme property which corresponds to a function used for the result processing. Therefore this property cannot be expressed as a formal mathematical property of a function. This property might be defined as a voting scheme property, but this would change neither the results nor the proofs. So we call it "a voting function property" for the sake of a convenient presentation.

Definition 7.6.2 (Private Voting Function). *A voting function F is private iff for any inputs $v_1, ..., v_N$, given the first $N - 1$ inputs and the result $R = F(v_1, ..., v_N)$, for any $A \in V$ it is impossible to prove that $v_N \neq A$.*

Example 7.6.1. Our example shows what a private voting function might look like. We assume that there are 100 voters, each votes "1" or "0". A function F summarizes the votes and maps the sum to a number from 0 to 9: If the sum is less or equal to 10, then the result of voting is 0; if the sum is larger than 10 but less or equal to 20, then the result of voting is 1 and so on:

$$R = F(V) = \sum_i \lceil v_i / 10 \rfloor$$

The function F satisfies all properties of a deterministic voting function.

Suppose only 15 out of the 100 voters vote with "1". The sum of the votes is 15, and the function F, by definition, produces the result $R = 1$. Conspiracy of any 99 voters can say nothing about the cast of the 100-th voter. No matter, what was the vote of the 100-th voter ("0" or "1"), the result would not change. And, by our presumption, nothing but a result is revealed.

Still, the voting function F is not private, because it does not preserve privacy for arbitrary input. Let the number of those who voted with "1" be 10. Then, the result of voting is 0. Now, consider any voter who voted with "0". The cooperation of the other 99 voters can realize his vote. More precisely, in this case, one can prove that the voter did not vote with "1", because if his cast were "1", then the result would change to 1.   □

7.6.2 Deterministic Voting Functions

First, we prove a theorem regarding a property any private deterministic voting function must have. Second, we prove that there are no deterministic voting functions that have that property.

To start with, we formally mention that we consider deterministic voting functions:

$$\not\exists \quad v_1, ..., v_N, \quad : \quad F(v_1, ..., v_N) \neq F(v_1, ..., v_N) \tag{7.5}$$

Theorem 7.6.1. (A Necessary Condition for a Private Deterministic Voting Function). *A voting function F is private only if*

$$\not\exists \quad v_1, ..., v_N, v_N' \quad : \quad F(v_1, ..., v_N) \neq F(v_1, ..., v_N') \tag{7.6}$$

We note that (7.6) is equivalent to

$$\forall \quad v_1, ..., v_N, v_N' \quad : \quad F(v_1, ..., v_N) = F(v_1, ..., v_N')$$

Proof. Assume, by contradiction, that some voting function F is private, and (7.6) does not hold:

$$\exists \ v_1, ..., v_N, v_N' \quad : \quad F(v_1, ..., v_N) \neq F(v_1, ..., v_N')$$

Let the casts be exactly $v_1, ..., v_N$. Thus, we have:

$$\exists \ v_N' \quad : \quad F(v_1, ..., v_N) \neq F(v_1, ..., v_N')$$

We conclude that $N - 1$ cooperating voters, who know their own votes $v_1, ..., v_{N-1}$ and the result of the voting R, can (due to (7.4)) compute $F(v_1, ..., v_{N-1}, x_N)$ for all the range of the values of a vote x_N. They find such an $x_N = v_N'$, that

$$F(v_1, ..., v_N') \neq R$$

From the property 7.5 of a deterministic function the cooperating voters conclude that $v_N' \neq v_N$. That is, they can prove that the N-th voter did not vote with v_N' value. (If there are only two possible values for votes, like "yes" or "no", they can even tell exactly what his vote was.) Formally, the coalition of $N - 1$ voters has the right to conclude that

$$v_N \neq v_N'$$

By definition 7.6.2, F is not a private function. Thus we have a contradiction.
□

Theorem 7.6.2. (Nonexistence of Private Deterministic Voting Function). *A deterministic voting function cannot be private.*

Proof. Assume that a private deterministic voting function F exists. Then the properties of a deterministic voting function (statements 7.2, 7.3, 7.4, 7.5) are true for F, and F satisfies the necessary condition of a private deterministic voting function (Theorem 7.6.1). Starting with this, we lead to a contradiction.

Let the casts of the voters be $v_1, ..., v_N$ and let the result be R:

$$F(v_1, ..., v_N) = R$$

STEP1. We can find the minimal number of voters j, that would change the result by changing their casts. Due to the voting function property 7.2, this number exists and it is less than or equal to N. Due to Theorem 7.6.1, this number must be more than 1:

$$\exists \ \underset{Theorem\ 7.6.1}{1 <} \ j \ \underset{Property\ 7.2}{\leqslant} \ N \quad :$$

$$\forall \ v_1^\star, ..., v_{j-1}^\star \quad : \quad F(v_1^\star, ..., v_{j-1}^\star, v_j, v_{j+1}..., v_N) = R \qquad (7.7)$$

$$\text{And} \ \exists \ v_1', ..., v_{j-1}', v_j' \quad : \quad F(v_1', ..., v_{j-1}', v_j', v_{j+1}, ..., v_N) \neq R \qquad (7.8)$$

STEP2. In (7.7), let us take $v_1^\star = v_1', ..., v_{j-1}^\star = v_{j-1}'$:

$$F(v_1', ..., v_{j-1}', v_j, v_{j+1}, ..., v_N) = R \qquad (7.9)$$

By combining (7.8) and (7.9), we get:

$$F(v_1', ..., v_{j-1}', v_j, v_{j+1}, ..., v_N) \neq F(v_1', ..., v_{j-1}', v_j', v_{j+1}, ..., v_N)$$

In the last expression, if we take into account property 7.3 of a voting function, then we get a contradiction to Theorem 7.6.1.   □

7.6.3 Probabilistic Voting Functions

We considered deterministic functions. Probabilistic functions are more general functions, in that they make possible different results with different probability for unique input.

In our notation, we define a probabilistic function by assigning a finite set of result–probability pairs for each possible set of casts (see Fig. 7.7). Considering the example where the result is calculated inside a secure coprocessor, a secure coprocessor simply outputs the result in accordance to given probability distributions.

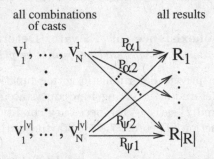

Fig. 7.7. Visual representation of a probabilistic function.

In this section we prove that although private voting is possible with probabilistic functions, any result is possible too. This statement might be viewed as a significant drawback for those who "make some use" of a result of an absolutely private voting.

From now on, whenever we refer to a voting function, or a private voting function, we mean a probabilistic voting function or a private probabilistic voting function, if not specified exactly.

7.6.3.1 Voting Function. First, we shortly rewrite the definitions of voting function properties because the notations are slightly changed to carry the notion of probability.

Property 1: Influence. Voters have an *influence* on the result of voting, i.e.

$$\forall v_1, ..., v_N, R \quad \exists j \leqslant N, v_1', ..., v_j' \quad :$$
$$P(R|v_1, ..., v_N) \neq P(R|v_1', ..., v_j', v_{j+1}, ..., v_N) \quad (7.10)$$

This property means that if the distribution is the same for any casts, this probabilistic function is not good for voting.

Property 2: Commutativity. Voters have an *equal* influence on the result of voting, i.e.

$$\forall v_1, ..., v_N, R, 1 \leqslant i < j \leqslant N \quad :$$
$$P(R|v_1, ..., v_i, ..., v_j, ..., v_N) = P(R|v_1, ..., v_j, ..., v_i, ..., v_N) \quad (7.11)$$

Property 3: Function Openness. Voters (or at least organizers) know how the votes are counted, i.e.

$$\text{One knows } P(R|v_1, ..., v_N) \text{ for any } R, v_1, ..., v_N . \quad (7.12)$$

7.6.3.2 Private Voting Function. We continue using the same definition of a private voting function as in the deterministic case (Definition 7.6.2).

Example 7.6.2. Let us start with the deterministic example given in Section 7.6.1. We might try to fix the problem in that example in the following way:

1. If the sum is not critical for privacy (like 1,2,3,4,5,6,7,8,9,12,13,14,15,...), we output the result as before: No privacy is revealed as we discussed. (Because, for these sums, changing one vote does not change the result.)
2. If the sum is critical (like 10 or 11), we run some probabilistic function that outputs results (like 0 or 1) with equal probability.

Suppose 11 voters voted with "1" and the result announced is 1, and 99 voters cooperate against the one (who voted with "1"). They cannot argue that his vote was "1" (as they do in the deterministic example) because he could voted with "0" (with the same probability), then the sum would be 10, but then it would be flipped to the result 1 due to our new voting function for critical sums.

Still, the described probabilistic voting function does not preserve privacy. Counterexample: Again, consider 11 voters who voted with "1" and the result announced is 0, and 99 voters cooperate against the one (who voted with "0"). They can argue, that his vote was not "1", because if it were "1", then the sum would be 12 and the result 0 would be impossible.

Below we prove formally that the private voting is still possible, but (considering this example) only if sometimes (very rarely) for all 100 votes "1" the result 0 appears, and (also very rarely) for all 100 votes "0" the result 9 appears. □

Theorem 7.6.3. (Existance of a Private Probabilistic Voting Function). *There exists a private probabilistic voting function.*

Proof. To prove the theorem, we give an example of a private probabilistic voting function. In other words, we give an example of a function that satisfies all three voting function properties listed before (statements 7.10, 7.11, 7.12) and that preserves absolute privacy of any voter (Definition 7.6.2).

There are 3 voters, two possible casts (0/1 or yes/no) and 4 different results (Fig. 7.8).

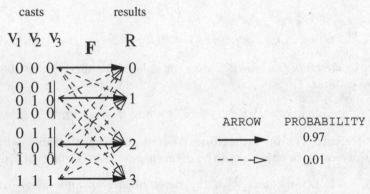

Fig. 7.8. An example of a private probabilistic voting function.

Clearly, the scheme might be generalized for any N, $|V|$ and $|R|$.

It also may be slightly adjusted so that the less the result corresponds to the set of casts, the smaller probability it has. In our case, for simplicity, all such probabilities are 0.01. □

It is remarkable that removing any single arrow makes the function not private. This is the subject of the next theorem.

The next theorem might be seen as a necessary condition for a function to be a private probabilistic voting function. It also shows how "poor" the voting functions must represent the result of a voting in order to provide absolute privacy. Roughly speaking, it proves that nobody can give an example of an absolutely private voting function, where for all 100 "yes" votes the result "no" is impossible.

Theorem 7.6.4. (The Flaw of a Private Probabilistic Voting Function). *Any private probabilistic voting function F has the following property:*

$$\forall R, v_1, ..., v_N \quad : \quad P_{F(v_1,...,v_N)=R} \neq 0 \qquad (7.13)$$

Proof. We give a very short proof, although it might be extended for better understanding.

Let us consider possible results (the probabilities are not zero) for the set of votes $v_1, ..., v_N$. We take one of these (possible) results - R. Starting with this, we prove that R has a non-zero probability for any other set of votes. This proves the theorem.

So, we have

$$P(R|v_1, ..., v_N) \neq 0$$

Then let us change one of the votes in the set to the arbitrary value. Let it be $v_N \longrightarrow v'_N$. Then we can write

$$P(R|v_1, ..., v'_N) \neq 0$$

If we cannot write the last equation, then, considering the equation before the last, we have absolute privacy definition violation, if the first $N-1$ voters cooperate against the N-th.

Using the same technique, by changing votes one by one, we achieve

$$P(R|v'_1, v'_2 ..., v'_N) \neq 0$$

□

7.6.4 Related Work

To our best knowledge, nothing in the related work tackles the problem setting we consider.

7.6.4.1 Secure Multi-Party Computation. Secure multi-party computation (SMPC) deals with computing *securely* any probabilistic function in a distributed network where each participant holds one of the inputs. "Securely" means that no more information is revealed to a participant than can be computed from that participant's input and a result [Gol99, GMW87]. Thus SMPC does not consider the question of how much information about a single input can be revealed in the result given the other inputs. Our work might be seen as a partial answer to this question.

7.6.4.2 Electronic Elections. In the research work on security and privacy in electronic elections (see [Coh86, Cha88, CGS97] for example), an enormous number of voting schemes have been proposed. The similarity between all those schemes is that in none of them the voter's privacy withstands an all-against-one attack. There is only one exception: Stochastic anonymous voting is discussed later in this section.

It seems that the hypothetical question of what it costs to protect the privacy of a single voter (or can it be protected at all) if all-but-one voters cooperate is not pondered even once.

Receipt-Free Voting. To stop vote buying, receipt-free voting [BT94, HS00] schemes are proposed that prevent (under such assumptions as "private booth" and "private channel" only) a voter from proving his cast to somebody else. So the all-against-one conspiracy of voters still may *know* the victim's vote, but they cannot *prove* it to somebody else. Because in order to prove it they should prove their own votes, which is made impossible by the receipt-freeness. Again, the question is not considered how a single vote might be protected if all other votes are somehow made known.

Stochastic Anonymous Voting. In [KAGN98] a stochastic voting protocol is proposed with the main idea that the voters have to randomize their votes before submitting them. A technique is also proposed of how organizers can force users to randomize their votes. Then, even if all votes are made known, the voters' privacy is preserved.

In that protocol, for any set of votes, any result is possible. However, the question is not considered whether there exists such an absolutely private voting scheme, that not all results are possible for any given set of votes[8]. Instead, some statistical properties of the protocol are investigated. And the primary result of that work is that the accuracy of the voting result improves as the number of voters increases.

Real Systems. There are a lot of voting systems implemented and offered by commercial companies. Some of them build their advertising campaigns on terms like "absolute privacy"[9]. What they probably mean is privacy under the assumption that an all-but-one conspiracy of voters is impossible.

7.6.4.3 Statistical Disclosure Control. The problem for a statistical database is how to preserve the privacy of individual data from anyone who wishes to get some statistics calculated on the set of several individual data [WdW96]. The absolutely private voting problem is different, since not only the result of the processing is known, but also all except one individual data are known too.

7.6.4.4 One-Way Hash Functions. One-way hash functions produce the result in a way that, given the result and not given some (even relatively small) part x_i of the input X, it is computationally difficult to say what is this hidden input x_i equal to [Sch96]. From the first point of view, such functions might be considered as private voting functions. They are not, because for one-way functions, although it is difficult to find $A: \quad x_i = A$, it costs nothing to find $A: \quad x_i \neq A$. And the latter is a privacy violation in case of voting.

---

[8] And the main achievement of our work is that we give and prove the *negative* answer to this question.

[9] "Our technology provides for absolute privacy of an individual's ballot ..." is officially claimed by one electronic voting company. Yet another company claims to provide "fail-safe" voter privacy, where fail-safe means that one cannot link a voter to a vote even if everyone colludes, etc.

7.6.4.5 Theories of Voting. The mathematics of voting (or, the theory of voting), in spite of being rather developed [Saa95], has nothing relevant to the problem we consider. One of the corner goals of the theory is to calculate votes so that the winner (one of more than two candidates) is "whom the voters really want" [Saa98]. In this context, an impossibility for some particular electoral systems [Woo87] is just one of the paradoxes known to the voting theory [Saa89, Nur99].

A probabilistic voting theory [Cou93] has a goal different from the voting theory. Probabilistic voting theory is the mathematical prediction of candidate behavior in, or in anticipation of, elections in which candidates are unsure of voters' preferences. This theory, as well as similar ones – spatial theory of voting [Ene84, EH90] and a unified theory of voting [SMG99], do not consider privacy questions.

7.6.4.6 No Voting – No Problem. Some work was dedicated to show that an election, as a main instrument of democracy, has many disadvantages. The basic one is that after the election occurs, a winner holds the promises no more. So, the election is just an illusion.

These disadvantages of an election might be removed just by avoiding elections. Interestingly, one insists that democracy is still well possible without elections [Mar96]. Instead of elections, other techniques are proposed to make decisions in the society.

Some of those techniques, like referendums[10], have the same mathematical model as elections, so the privacy problem remains. Other alternatives are completely different from normal elections, so that the notion of privacy is meaningless for them. One of the most radical alternatives (the sortition) is to take randomly one of all allowed outcomes as a result [CM99].

7.6.5 Discussion

We clarify some questionable points of the presented material.

7.6.5.1 The Absolutely Private Voting Scheme Proposed. From some perspective, using the absolutely private voting function we proposed in Theorem 3 is not very different from picking candidates at random. And so, one might conclude the proposed voting scheme is useless.

The proposed voting scheme is a side-effect of our work. So we do not discuss much about whether this system is good for voting or not - this is done very well by Kikuchi et al. [KAGN98] using the probability theory. Our main result is a proof of the paradoxical statement: If one wants to build an absolutely private voting system, he can do no better than (accidentally very similar) our or Kikuchi et al. [KAGN98] scheme.

---

[10] Instead of electing politicians who then make policy decisions, these decisions are made directly by the public voting [Mar96].

7.6.5.2 The Definition of Voting Function. Our definition of a voting function is very general. Basically, it is any non-constant function. The question is whether we should define it more strictly. We think that the more general the functions we consider to prove the theorems, the more universal these theorems are.

For example, we could improve the definition of a voting function by saying that the voting function should indicate undoubtedly if the majority (or generally, a given amount) of voters voted for a proposition. But it follows directly from Theorem 4 that such improved voting functions cannot be private. It is also evident that if we substitute "undoubtedly" for "with high probability" then such private functions exist.

7.6.6 The Implication of Absolute Privacy

In this section we summarize our results on absolute privacy in voting. Voting is absolutely private if a voter can insist that he voted with an arbitrary cast (to preserve his privacy) and nobody (in any conspiracy) can prove that he lies.

Our goal was to investigate whether or not absolute privacy is possible. And if it is possible, then under which conditions. We considered special types of functions that are likely to reflect the most important properties of any voting. For these functions, we proved that absolute privacy holds only if the voting function is probabilistic and for any set of casts any result is possible.

In summary, absolute privacy has a price. It is up to the participants to decide whether they want the "real" result or "real" privacy. It is impossible to have both simultaneously[11]. We have shown that there is a tradeoff between the absolute privacy of a vote and the precision of a result of the voting.

7.7 Summary

In the PIR model, distributing royalties between the owners of records would require revealing information about user queries. However, revealing information about queries is prohibited by the PIR model.

We showed how to distribute the royalties while violating user privacy as little as possible. Namely, based on the concept of the repudiation property introduced in the previous chapter, we demonstrated a protocol that distributes the royalties while preserving the repudiation property of the users. Furthermore, we showed how the precision of our royalty distribution scheme depends on the robustness of the repudiation provided.

---

[11] This might be seen as a self-contradiction of democracy: Privacy and voting are two important aspects of democracy. But we have shown that they cannot perfectly coexist, i.e., one or the other must inherently be flawed.

We identified a certain negative property of the royalty distribution scheme. We also observed that a similar property belongs to any electronic voting scheme that preserves user privacy. We then switched the context from DRM/RIR to electronic voting, and proved that this property cannot be avoided. This result contributes to the state of the art in the area of electronic voting.

Part IV

Discussion

8 Conclusion and Future Work

This chapter summarizes the book by recalling the results of our research, and by pointing out possible directions for future research.

8.1 Summary

> ... This example shows that
> algorithms, like computer hardware, are a *technology*.
> – *Cormen, Leiserson, Rivest, [CLR90], page 16*

Private Information Retrieval (PIR) is the problem of retrieving a single record from a server's database of N records such that the server gathers no information about the identity of the record.

Previous work on PIR was dedicated to answering several theoretical questions, without paying attention to such practical characteristics as query response time. This oversight resulted in solutions with low or intolerable performance. The simple model of the PIR allows one to study this problem very formally. However, the solutions that fully satisfy this simple model are difficult to apply to real world problems.

The main contribution of this work is twofold: On the one hand, we designed a PIR solution that outperforms the currently existing PIR approaches by far, making an application of PIR practically feasible. On the other hand, we generalized the PIR model such that it better fits the real world, thus making our solutions even more practical. We call this book "querying databases privately" to emphasize that our main goal is to perform research respected not only by the security community, but by the database community as well.

We briefly enumerate each of the subproblems that we solved in order to make PIR practical.

1. **An efficient solution for the common PIR model.** Our first contribution is a PIR protocol whose communication complexity and query response time are independent of the number of records in the database.

D. Asonov: Querying Databases Privately, LNCS 3128, 101–105, 2004.

a) $O(1)$ **Query response time and** $O(1)$ **communication.** The initially proposed solutions can be divided in two categories. The first (and the largest) category of solutions aims at reducing communication between the server and the user; the best solution is based on a secure coprocessor, and attains $O(1)$ communication complexity. However, all the solutions of the first category offer a query response time of $O(N)$ complexity, which is intolerable in many practical cases. The second category of solutions provides $O(1)$ query response time by employing preprocessing. However, an amount of information comparable to the size of the database must be transferred from the server to the client before the protocol can start. Our approach possesses the advantages of both categories, but avoids their drawbacks. Namely, we designed a PIR protocol that has $O(1)$ communication and $O(1)$ query response time, and requires no pre-communication. Additionally, we formally prove the privacy property of our protocol using the concept of maximal entropy from Shannon's theory of information.

b) **Efficient shuffling algorithm.** Our approach employs preprocessing, as any PIR protocol with query response time less than $O(N)$ must do. The preprocessing, in our case, consists of shuffling the database using a secure coprocessor, such that the server does not know the identities of the records anymore. A single shuffled database can be used to answer only a limited number of queries, which means that the preprocessing must be performed periodically. Initially we proposed a shuffling algorithm (SSA) that performs $O(N^2)$ I/Os in order to shuffle a database. However, even rough theoretical estimations show that this complexity will result in days or even weeks of preprocessing time. Therefore, we designed SSG – a shuffling algorithm whose complexity we initially estimated to be $O(N^{1.5})$. Taking into account that reading a database completely requires $O(N)$ I/Os, a database shuffling algorithm of $O(N^{1.5})$ complexity can be considered to be nearly optimal.

c) **Experimental evaluation of shuffling algorithms.** There is an alternative shuffling algorithm that we discovered later in related work. This algorithm (we denote it by SBS), is based on the bitonic sorting network, and requires $O(Nlog^2N)$ I/Os to shuffle a database. The complexities of the SSG and SBS lie relatively near each other. Additionally, these complexities are both presented in $O()$ notation. Therefore, even one order of difference in the factor (hidden under $O()$ notation) may determine whether SSG or SBS is superior. We implemented SSA, SSG and SBS and used an available secure coprocessor to evaluate these protocols experimentally. In our tests, SSG outperforms SBS by approximately one order of magnitude. This observation, together with other experimental data, revealed that our initial theoretical calculations ($O(N^{1.5})$) underestimate the performance of SSG. We took a closer look at the estimation of SSG complexity and discovered that $O(N^{1.5})$ is only an upper boundary for its complexity. More precisely, the complexity of SSG varies between $O(N^{1.5})$ and $O(N)$, depending on database parameters such as the size of the records and the number of records (N). SSG employs many I/O operations with fractions of a record, and the smaller the record the slower the disk's and SC's I/Os. Generally speaking, SSG approaches $O(N)$ complexity either for large enough records or if the random access memory is used instead of the secondary storage and a SC is optimized for short I/Os.

2. **Elaborating the PIR model.** The second part of our results elaborates the PIR model in order to make it more flexible and practically applicable. There are two generalizations of the PIR model that we proposed and investigated.

   a) **Relaxed privacy definition (repudiation).** All of the PIR protocols from related work only consider full privacy. Our first generalization introduces the notion of relaxed privacy (repudiation). We construct protocols that provide such privacy in order to offer the user a trade-off between the level of privacy and the complexity of the protocol. Before constructing protocols that provide relaxed privacy, we faced the problem of *defining* relaxed privacy and quantitatively *measuring* its robustness. An additional obstacle was that Shannon's measure of revealed information is not applicable as a measure of the relaxed privacy for our case. Applying the same approach as Shannon used to define his measure of information, we formulated a set of conditions that must hold for the measure of relaxed privacy. We then postulated that every function that satisfies these conditions is suitable for measuring the robustness of relaxed privacy, or robustness of repudiation for short.

   b) **Repudiative information retrieval (RIR).** Based on the definition of repudiation, we initially built a protocol that provides repudiation, but this repudiation was only of a particular robustness. Next, we extended our protocol to provide an arbitrary robustness in the range from 0 (no repudiation) to 1 (full robustness of repudiation). Naturally, the RIR protocol that provides full robustness of repudiation resembles a PIR protocol, thus providing no advantages (in this case) over PIR. However, if the user is ready to sacrifice some privacy for better performance of the protocol, then RIR protocols come into play, providing performance that none of the existing PIR protocol has succeeded in demonstrating. We formally exposed the exact relationship between the complexity of our RIR protocol and the robustness of the repudiation provided.

c) **Distribution of royalties.** Our second generalization removes the assumption that there is only one owner of digital goods stored in the database. We consider the problem of distributing royalties between the owners of digital goods depending on how many retrievals of each record took place. The challenge we had to overcome was that PIR requires no information to be revealed about the content of the queries. Thus, no information would be available for the server to use in deciding how to distribute royalties. We employed our previous research on relaxed privacy, which we called repudiation, to allow some information about queries to be revealed for use in royalty distribution. However, this information should be revealed in a way that the repudiation property is preserved. We demonstrated a royalty distribution scheme that fulfills this requirement. Furthermore, we identified that any royalty distribution scheme that provides repudiation property for the users also produces a certain sort of inaccuracy in the distribution of royalties. We proved that this drawback is unavoidable. Surprisingly, this negative result can also be interpreted in the context of another research area – electronic voting.

8.2 Future Work

> Dissertations are not finished; they are abandoned.
> – *Frederick P. Brooks, Turing award recipient*

This section discusses problems that are associated with querying databases privately, but go beyond the scope of this book. Solving any of these problems would continue the research presented in this book.

8.2.1 Querying Databases Privately without Tamper-Resistant Hardware

Most of the algorithms proposed in this book utilize a secure coprocessor – a device that runs programs while ensuring that it is not tampered with. Our protocols require a secure coprocessor at the server's (service provider's) site only (and *no* secure coprocessor for clients is needed), which is still a limitation.

It remains an open issue to prove formally that this limitation is unavoidable, or to find practical algorithms that run without (or with negligible assistance of) a tamper-resistant device installed on the server.

We provide two starting points for this direction of research.

1. Anderson, being one of the leading experts in the security community, points out that the widely accepted statement "everything in hardware can be implemented in software" may not be the case with secure co-processors, in principle ([And01], p.278). However, the exact distinction between what can be done by a secure coprocessor and what can be done by software has not been drawn yet. Finding and formally stating this distinction may help to clarify whether or not a SC is the only option for querying databases privately.

2. In contrast to the *general-purpose* hardware, a secure coprocessor is a type of *special* hardware, meaning it is not sold with every computer server by default. An interesting direction would be to look for solutions that employ general-purpose hardware instead of the special hardware. More precisely, one might try to use emerging general-purpose tamper-resistant technologies (like Compaq, HP, IBM, Intel and Microsoft's initiative called TCPA [And02] or Transmeta's initiative [Cor03]) to construct protocols such as PIR. An obvious barrier in this direction is that the emerging general-purpose tamper-resistant hardware is slower and less secure, at least at the present time.

8.2.2 Elaborate Query–Database Models

We have made two efforts to extend the PIR model as described in Chapters 6 and 7. However, we believe that it might be of practical interest to further extend and elaborate the PIR model. For example, an extension of the set of supported query types is needed if we want to offer the user the capability to fire not only queries of the type "return the i-th record" but also of the type "What books of Po Bronson do you have in your digital store?".

This exact type of query appears to be of particular necessity for practical applications, because very often the user must run a search query to find the record of his interest before actually retrieving this record from the database.

Although we believe that this case requires additional investigation, there are two straightforward approaches that allow the user to search privately. One approach is to download the catalog (of patent abstracts or book descriptions) and to browse it locally. Another approach is to execute search queries with a SC on the server, by applying our approach of querying records privately to access a search index.

A similar, but more complicated task is constructing an efficient Internet search engine that allows the users to search privately.

References

[AC02]   Dmitri Asonov and Don Coppersmith. Private communication, November 2002.

[AD02]   Dmitri Asonov and Neil K. Daswani. Personal communication, November 2002.

[AF01]   Dmitri Asonov and Johann-Christoph Freytag. Almost optimal private information retrieval. Technical Report HUB-IB-156, Humboldt University Berlin, November 2001.

[AF02a]   Dmitri Asonov and Johann-Christoph Freytag. Almost optimal private information retrieval. In *Proceedings of 2nd Workshop on Privacy Enhancing Technologies (PET2002), San Francisco, USA*, April 2002.

[AF02b]   Dmitri Asonov and Johann-Christoph Freytag. Private information retrieval, optimal for users and secure coprocessors. Technical Report HUB-IB-159, Humboldt University Berlin, May 2002.

[AF02c]   Dmitri Asonov and Johann-Christoph Freytag. Repudiative information retrieval. In *Proceedings of the 1st ACM Workshop on Privacy in the Electronic Society (WPES2002), Washington DC, USA*, November 2002.

[Afa76]   Alexander Afanas'ev. *Russian Fairy Tales*. Random House, October 1976.

[AFK89]   Martin Abadi, Joan Feigenbaum, and Joe Kilian. On hiding information from an oracle. *Journal of Computer and System Sciences*, 39(1):21–50, 1989.

[AKS83]   Miklós Ajtai, János Komlos, and Endre Szemeradi. An $o(nlogn)$ sorting network. In *Proceedings of the 25-th ACM Symposium on Theory of Computing*, 1983.

[AKSX02]   Rakesh Agrawal, Jerry Kiernan, Ramakrishnan Srikant, and Yirong Xu. Hippocratic databases. In *Proceedings of the 28th VLDB Conference, Hong Kong, China*, August 2002.

[Amb97]   Andris Ambainis. Upper bound on the communication complexity of private information retrieval. In *Proceedings of 24th ICALP*, 1997.

[And01]   Ross Anderson. *Security Engineering*. Wiley, 2001.

[And02]   Ross Anderson. Tcpa / palladium frequently asked questions. http://www.cl.cam.ac.uk/~rja14/tcpa-faq.html, July 2002.

[AS02]   Dmitri Asonov and Sean Smith. Private communication, April 2002.

[ASF01]   Dmitri Asonov, Markus Schaal, and Johann-Christoph Freytag. Absolute privacy in voting. In *Proceedings of Information Security Conference 2001, Malaga, Spain*, October 2001.

[Aso01]   Dmitri Asonov. Private information retrieval - an overview and current trends. In *Proceedings of the ECDPvA Workshop, Informatik 2001, Vienna, Austria*, September 2001.

[Bat68]   Kenneth E. Batcher. Sorting networks and their applications. In *Proceedings of AFIPS Spring Joint Comput. Conference, Vol.32*, 1968.

[BCR86]   Gilles Brassard, Claude Crépeau, and J. Robert. All-or-nothing disclosure of secrets. In *Proceedings of Crypto'86*, 1986.

[BDF00]   Feng Bao, Robert H. Deng, and Peirong Feng. An efficient and practical scheme for privacy protection in the e-commerce of digital goods. In *Proceedings of the 3rd International Conference on Information Security and Cryptology*, December 2000.

[BDS00]   Carlo Blundo, Paolo D'Arco, and Alfredo De Santis. A t-private k-database information retrieval scheme. *International J. of Information Security*, July 2000. http://dx.doi.org/10.1007/s102070100005.

[Bea00]   Caroline Beaumont. What price privacy when dotcoms go down? *NEW ZEALAND HERALD*, September 2000.

[BF90]   Donald Beaver and Joan Feigenbaum. Hiding instances in multioracle queries. In *Proceedings of the 7th STACS, LNCS Vol. 415, Springer Verlag*, 1990.

[BFG02]   Richard Beigel, Lance Fortnow, and William Gasarch. Nearly tight bounds for private information retrieval systems. Technical Note 2002-L001N, NEC Laboratories America., 2002.

[BFKR91]   Donald Beaver, Joan Feigenbaum, Joe Kilian, and Phillip Rogaway. Security with low communication overhead. In *Proceedings of CRYPTO'90, Springer-Verlag*, pages 62–76, 1991.

[BI01]   Amos Beimel and Yuval Ishai. Information-theoretic private information retrieval: A unified construction. ECCC Report TR01-015, February 2001.

[BIKM99]   Amos Beimel, Yuval Ishai, Eyal Kushilevitz, and Tal Malkin. One-way functions are essential for single-server private information retrieval. In *Proceedings of 31st STOC*, 1999.

[BIKR02]   Amos Beimel, Yuval Ishai, Eyal Kushilevitz, and Jean-Francois Raymond. Breaking the $o(n^{1/(2k-1)})$ barrier for information-theoretic private information retrieva. In *Proceedings of the 43rd IEEE Symposium on Foundations of Computer Science (FOCS), Vancouver, Canada*, November 2002.

[BIM00]   Amos Beimel, Yuval Ishai, and Tal Malkin. Reducing the servers computation in private information retrieval: PIR with preprocessing. In *Proceedings of CRYPTO'00*, 2000.

[BS02]   Amos Beimel and Yoav Stahl. Robust information-theoretic private information retrieval. In *Proceedings of the 3rd Conference on Security in Communication Networks, Amalfi, Italy*, September 2002.

[BT94]   Josh Benaloh and Dwight Tuinstra. Receipt-free secret-ballot elections. In *Proceedings of the 26th ACM Symposium on Theory of Computing*, pages 544–553, May 1994.

[CDNO97]   Ran Canetti, Cynthia Dwork, Moni Naor, and Rafail Ostrovsky. Deniable encryption. In *Proceedings of Advances in Cryptology, (CRYPTO-97)*, June 1997.

[CF85]   Josh D. Cohen and Michael J. Fischer. A robust and verifiable cryptographically secure election scheme. In *Proceedings of 26th FOCS*, 1985.

[CFSY96]   Ronald Cramer, Matthew Franklin, Berry Schoenmakers, and Moti Yung. Multi-authority secret-ballot elections with linear work. In *Proceedings of EUROCRYPT'96, LNCS 1070*, 1996.

[CG97]   Benny Chor and Niv Gilboa. Computationally private information retrieval. In *Proceedings of 29th STOC*, 1997.

[CGKS95] Benny Chor, Oded Goldreich, Eyal Kushilevitz, and Madhu Sudan. Private information retrieval. In *Proceedings of 36th FOCS*, 1995.

[CGN97]   Benny Chor, Niv Gilboa, and Moni Naor. Private information retrieval by keywords. Technical report, Technion: Israel Institute of Technology, 1997.

[CGS97]   Ronald Cramer, Rosario Gennaro, and Berry Schoenmakers. A secure and optimally efficient multi-authority election scheme. In *Theory and Application of Cryptographic Techniques*, pages 103–118, 1997.

[Cha81]   David Chaum. Untraceable electronic mail, return addresses, and digital pseudonyms. *Communications of the ACM*, 24(2):84–88, February 1981.

[Cha88]   David Chaum. Elections with unconditionally-secret ballots and disruption equivalent to breaking RSA. In *Advances in Cryptology: Proc. of EuroCrypt'88, LNCS 330, SpringerVerlag*, pages 177–182, May 1988.

[CIO98]   Giovanni Di Crescenzo, Yuval Ishai, and Rafail Ostrovsky. Universal service-providers for database private information retrieval. In *Proceedings of 17th PODC*, 1998.

[CLR90]   Thomas H. Cormen, Charles E. Leiserson, and Ronald L. Rivest. *Introduction to Algorithms*. MIT Press, Cambridge, Massachusetts, 1990.

[CM99]   Lyn Carson and Brian Martin. *Random selection in politics*. Praeger, 1999.

[CMO00]   Giovanni Di Crescenzo, Tal Malkin, and Rafail Ostrovsky. Single database private information retrieval implies oblivious transfer. In *EUROCRYPT 2000, volume 1807 of LNCS*, pages 122–138, 2000.

[CMS99]   Christian Cachin, Silvio Micali, and Markus Stadler. Computationally private information retrieval with polylogarithmic communication. In *Proceedings of EUROCRYPT'99*, 1999.

[CNN00]   CNN. Amazon client checks out. *CNN Financial Network*, http://cnnfn.cnn.com/2000/09/13/technology/privacy/index.htm, September 2000.

[Coh86]   Josh Cohen. Improving privacy in cryptographic elections. Technical Report 454, Yale University, Department of Computer Science, February 1986.

[Cor03]   Transmeta Corporation. Transmeta announces first embedded security features for x86 microprocessors (press release). http://investor. transmeta.com/news/20030114-99407.cfm, January 2003.

[Cou93]   Peter J. Coughlin. *Probabilistic Voting Theory*. Cambridge University Press, February 1993.

[CY01]   Hsiao Clement Chun-Yun. Private information retrieval does not imply one-way permutations. Master's thesis, National Taiwan University, 2001.

[Dis00]   Jennifer Disabatino. Disney offers to buy toysmart.com customer list. *CNN News Online*, http://www.cnn.com/2000/TECH/computing/ 07/14/disney.toysmart.list.idg/, June 2000.

[DLP+01] Joan G. Dyer, Mark Lindemann, Ronald Perez, Reiner Sailer, Leendert van Doorn, Sean W. Smith, and Steve Weingart. Building the ibm 4758 secure coprocessor. *IEEE Computer*, 34(10):57–66, October 2001.

[DSCP02] Claudia Diaz, Stefaan Seys, Joris Claessens, and Bart Preneel. Towards measuring anonymity. In *Proceedings of 2nd Workshop on Privacy Enhancing Technologies (PET2002), San Francisco, USA*, April 2002.

[EH90]   James M. Enelow and Melvin J. Hinich, editors. *Advances in the Spatial Theory of Voting*. Cambridge University Press, September 1990.

[Ene84]   James M. Enelow, editor. *Spatial Theory of Voting*. Cambridge University Press, 1984.

[Ger00]   Ed Gerck. Internet voting requirements. *The Bell*, 1(7):3–5,11–13, November 2000.

[GGM98]   Yael Gertner, Shafi Goldwasser, and Tal Malkin. A random server model for private information retrieval. In *Proceedings of 2nd RANDOM*, 1998.

[GIKM98]   Yael Gertner, Yuval Ishai, Eyal Kushilevitz, and Tal Malkin. Protecting data privacy in private information retrieval schemes. In *Proceedings of 30th STOC*, 1998.

[Gil00]   Niv Gilboa. *Topics in Private Information Retrieval*. PhD thesis, Technion - Israel Institute of Technology, 2000.

[GKST02]   Oded Goldreich, Howard Karloff, Leonard J. Schulman, and Luca Trevisan. Lower bounds for linear locally decodable codes and private information retrieval. In *Proceedings of 17th IEEE Annual Conference on Computational Complexity, Montreal, Canada*, May 2002.

[GM84]   Shafi Goldwasser and Silvio Micali. Probabilistic encryption. *Journal of Computer and System Sciences*, 1984.

[GMW87]   Oded Goldreich, Silvio Micali, and Avi Wigderson. How to play any mental game or a completeness theorem for protocols with honest majority. In *Proceedings of STOC'87*, May 1987.

[GO96]   Oded Goldreich and Rafail Ostrovsky. Software protection and simulation on oblivious rams. *Journal of ACM*, 43(3), May 1996.

[Gol99]   Oded Goldreich. Preface to special issue on general secure multi-party computation. `http://www.wisdom.weizmann.ac.il/~oded/PS/preSI.ps`, October 1999.

[GS02]   Alison Gibbs and Francis Edward Su. On choosing and bounding probability metrics. *International Statistical Review*, 70(3), December 2002.

[HS00]   Martin Hirt and Kazue Sako. Efficient receipt-free voting based on homomorphic encryption. In Bart Preneel, editor, *Advances in Cryptology – EUROCRYPT'00*, volume 1807 of *Lecture Notes in Computer Science*, pages 539–556. Springer-Verlag, May 2000.

[IK99]   Yuval Ishai and Eyal Kushilevitz. Improved upper bounds on information-theoretic private information retrieval. In *Proceedings of 31st STOC*, pages 79–88, 1999.

[Ito99]   Toshiya Itoh. Efficient private information retrieval. *IEICE Transactions*, E82-A(1):11–20, January 1999.

[Ito01]   Toshiya Itoh. On lower bounds for the communication complexity of private information retrieval. *IEICE Transactions*, E84-A(1), January 2001.

[Jay94]   Edwin Thompson Jaynes. *Probability theory: the logic of science.* `http://omega.math.albany.edu:8008/JaynesBook.html`, 1994.

[Jue01]   Ari Juels. Targeted advertising... and privacy too. In *Proceedings of RSA*, April 2001.

[KAGN98]   Hiroaki Kikuchi, Jin Akiyama, Howard Gobioff, and Gisaku Nakamura. Stochastic anonymous voting. Technical Report CMU-CS-98-112, Carnegie Mellon University, February 1998.

[KdW02]   Iordanis Kerenidis and Ronald de Wolf. Exponential lower bound for 2-query locally decodable codes via a quantum argument. In *Proceedings of Electronic Colloquium on Computational Complexity (ECCC), Vol. 9*, 2002.

[Knu81]   Donald E. Knuth. *The art of computer programming*, volume 2. Addison-Wesley, second edition, Jan 1981.

[KO97]   Eyal Kushilevitz and Rafail Ostrovsky. Replication is NOT needed: Single-database computationally private information retrieval. In *Proceedings of 38th FOCS*, 1997.

[KO00]   Eyal Kushilevitz and Rafail Ostrovsky. One-way trapdoor permutations are sufficient for single-database computationally-private information retrieval. In *EUROCRYPT 2000, volume 1807 of LNCS*, 2000.

[KY01]   Aggelos Kiayias and Moti Yung. Secure games with polynomial expressions. In *Proceedings of 28th ICALP*, 2001.

[LS01]   Mark Lindemann and Sean W. Smith. Improving des coprocessor throughput for short operations. In *Proceedings of 10th USENIX Security Symposium, Washington D.C., USA*, August 2001.

[Mac00]   David J.C. MacKay. *Textbook on Information Theory.* http://wol.ra.phy.cam.ac.uk/mackay/Book.html, 2000.

[Mal00]   Tal Malkin. *A Study of Secure Database Access and General Two-Party computation.* PhD thesis, Cryptography and Information Security Group, Laboratory for Computer Science, MIT, February 2000.

[Man98]   Eran Mann. Private access to distributed information. Master's thesis, Technion - Israel Institute of Technology, 1998.

[Mar96]   Brian Martin. Democracy without elections. *Social Anarchism*, (21):18–51, 1995-96.

[Mis00]   Sanjeev Kumar Mishra. *On Symmetrically Private Information Retrieval.* PhD thesis, Indian Statistical Institute, Calcutta, August 2000.

[MS00]   Sanjeev Kumar Mishra and Palash Sarkar. Symmetrically private information retrieval (extended abstract). In *Proceedings of INDOCRYPT, LNCS 1977*, December 2000.

[NP99a]   Moni Naor and Benny Pinkas. Oblivious transfer and polynomial evaluation. In *Proceedings of the 31th Annu. ACM Symp. on the Theory of Computing*, 1999.

[NP99b]   Moni Naor and Benny Pinkas. Oblivious transfer with adaptive queries. In *Advances in Cryptology – CRYPTO'99, volume 1666 of LNCS, Springer-Verlag*, pages 573–590, 1999.

[Nur99]   Hannu Nurmi. *Voting Paradoxes and How to Deal with Them.* Springer-Verlag, 1999.

[Ols99]   Stefanie Olsen. Top web sites compromise consumer privacy. *CNET News Archive,* http://yahoo.cnet.com/news/0-1007-200-1500309.html, December 1999.

[OS97]   Rafail Ostrovsky and Victor Shoup. Private information storage. In *Proceedings of 29th STOC*, 1997.

[Per02]   Ronald Perez. Private communication, November 2002.

[Rab81]   Michael O. Rabin. How to exchange secrets by oblivious transfer. Technical Report TR-81, Aiken Computation Laboratory, Harvard, 1981.

[Ray00]   Jean-François Raymond. Private information retrieval: Improved upper bound, extension and applications. Master's thesis, School of Computer Science, McGill University, Montreal, December 2000.

[Riv98]   Ronald L. Rivest. Chaffing and winnowing: Confidentiality without encryption. http://theory.lcs.mit.edu/~rivest/chaffing.txt, April 1998.

[Rot99]   Mark Rotenber. The online privacy protection act. *Electronic Privacy Information Center,* http://www.epic.org/privacy/internet/EPIC_testimony_799.pdf, July 1999.

[RS00]   Keith Regan and Clare Saliba. Privacy watchdogs blast amazon. *E Commerce Times,* http://www.ecommercetimes.com/news/articles2000/000914-3.shtml, September 2000.

[Saa89]   Donald G. Saari. A dictionary for voting paradoxes. *Journal of Economic Theory*, (48):443–475, 1989.

[Saa95]   Donald G. Saari. *Basic Geometry of Voting*. Springer-Verlag, December 1995.

[Saa98]   Donald G. Saari. Geometry, voting, and paradoxes. *Mathematics Magazine*, (78):243–259, October 1998.

[San00]   Greg Sandoval. Failed dot-coms may be selling your private information. *CNET News Archive*,
           http://yahoo.cnet.com/news/0-1007-200-2176430.html, June 2000.

[Sch96]   Bruce Schneier. *Applied Cryptography*. Wiley, New York, 2nd edition, 1996.

[SD02]   Andrei Serjantov and George Danezis. Towards an information theoretic metric for anonymity. In *Proceedings of 2nd Workshop on Privacy Enhancing Technologies (PET2002), San Francisco, USA*, April 2002.

[SH02]   Vitaly Shmatikov and Dominic J.D. Hughes. Defining anonymity and privacy. In *Proceedings of Workshop on Issues in the Theory of Security (WITS '02)*, January 2002.

[Sha48]   Shannon. A mathematical theory of communication. *Bell Systems Technical Journal*, 27, 1948.

[Shm02]   Vitaly Shmatikov. Probabilistic analysis of anonymity. In *Proceedings of 15th IEEE Computer Security Foundations Workshop (CSFW)*, June 2002.

[SJ00]   Claus Peter Schnorr and Markus Jakobsson. Security of signed elgamal encryption. In *Proceedings of ASIACRYPT'00, LNCS 1976*, December 2000.

[SMG99]   III Samuel Merrill and Bernard Grofman. *A Unified Theory of Voting*. Cambridge University Press, November 1999.

[Smi00]   Sean W. Smith. Webalps: Using trusted co-servers to enhance privacy and security of web transactions. IBM Research Report RC-21851, IBM T.J. Watson Research Center, October 2000.

[SPW98]   Sean W. Smith, Elaine R. Palmer, and Steve H. Weingart. Using a high-performance, programmable secure coprocessor. In *Proceedings of the 2nd International Conference on Financial Cryptography*, February 1998.

[SS99]   Paul F. Syverson and Stuart G. Stubblebine. Group principals and the formalization of anonymity. In *Proceedings of World Congress on Formal Methods*, September 1999.

[SS00]   Sean W. Smith and Dave Safford. Practical private information retrieval with secure coprocessors. Technical report, IBM Research Division, T. J. Watson Research Center, July 2000.

[SS01]   Sean W. Smith and Dave Safford. Practical server privacy with secure coprocessors. *IBM Systems Journal*, 40(3), September 2001.

[ST97]   Tomas Sander and Christian F. Tschudin. Towards mobile cryptography. Technical Report TR-97-049, International Computer Science Institute, Berkeley, November 1997.

[WdW96]   Leon Willenborg and Ton de Waal. *Statistical Disclosure Control in Practice*, volume 111 of *Lecture Notes in Statistics*. Springer-Verlag, 1996.

[Wie00]   Gio Wiederhold. Private communication, June 2000.

[Woo87]   Douglas R. Woodall. An impossibility theorem for electoral systems. *Discrete Mathematics*, (66):209–211, 1987.

[Yam01]   Akihiro Yamamura. Private information retrieval scheme based on the subgroup membership problem. Symposium on Cryptography and Information Security, January 2001.

[Yee94]   Bennet S. Yee. *Using Secure Coprocessors*. PhD thesis, Carnegie Mellon Univerisity, May 1994.

[YXB02]   Erica Y. Yang, Jie Xu, and Keith H. Bennett. Private information retrieval in the presence of malicious faults. In *Proceedings of 26th IEEE International Conference on Computer Software and Applications (COMPSAC2002), Oxford, England*, August 2002.

Index

Batcher's sort, *see* SBS
bitonic sort, *see* SBS

Compaq, 105

DBIS, vi
defense applications, 9
democracy, 95
DFG, vi
distance, 72
DRM, 77

economics
   associated with PIR, vi, 77
encryption
   deniable, 72
   homomorphic, 18
entropy, *see* Shannon's theory

FIPS, 85

GRK, vi

HP, 105

IBM, vi, 105
IBM 4758, *see* secure coprocessor, 50, 55
Intel, 50, 105

Linux, 50

measure
   of information revealed, 30, *see* Shannon's theory
   of robustness of repudiation, *see* robustness of repudiation
Microsoft, 105
morphing, 63

PCI, 50
PIR
   definition
      formal, 30
      informal, 4
      non-trivial, 13

   of blocks, 13
   quantum, 13

recycling, 42, *see* shuffling algorithms
repudiation, 59
   property, 60
   robustness of, 62
reshuffling, *see* shuffling algorithms
RIR, 59
   definition, 60
RR, *see* repudiation

SBS, *see* shuffling
SC, *see* secure coprocessor
secure coprocessor, 15
secure multi-party computation, 18, 93
Shannon, *see* theory
shuffling
   algorithm, 24
      SBS, 49
      SSA, 24
      SSG, 38
   experimental analysis, 49
SMPC, *see* secure multi-party computation
SQL, 5
SSA, *see* shuffling
SSG, *see* shuffling

tamper-resistance, *see* secure coprocessor
TCPA, 105
theory
   information, *see* Shannon's
   probability, 62, 95
   Shannon's, 30
   voting, 95
Transmeta, 105
trustworthiness, v

unpredictability, *see* Shannon's theory

zero information revealed, 30, 66, *see* Shannon's theory

D. Asonov: Querying Databases Privately, LNCS 3128, p. 115, 2004.
© Springer-Verlag Berlin Heidelberg 2004

Lecture Notes in Computer Science

For information about Vols. 1–3029

please contact your bookseller or Springer-Verlag